Theme Kits Made Easy

Leslie Silk Eslinger

Redleaf Press
St. Paul, Minnesota
www.redleafpress.org

Chapter opening illustrations by Kathy Kruger
Toy librarian illustrations by Jane Keer-Keer

Published by: Redleaf Press
           a division of Resources for Child Caring
           450 N. Syndicate, Suite 5
           St. Paul, MN 55104

Library of Congress Cataloging-in-Publication Data

Eslinger, Leslie Silk, 1946–
   Theme kits made easy / by Leslie Silk Eslinger.
       p. cm.
Includes bibliographical references.
   ISBN 1-929610-26-2 (pbk.)
   1. Unit method of teaching. 2. Education, Preschool—Activity
programs. 3. Teaching—Aids and devices. I. Title.
   LB1029.U6 E84 2002
   372.133—dc21
                                                2002008794

To Rick, Julia, Leah, and Ilene, who together gave me the confidence to see this through!

To Leah, my poem assistant.

To Jul, who chuckled at the poems.

To Ilene, my cheerleader.

To Jen, who made me feel special.

And to Rick, for organizing me, dotting my i's, and putting my mind at ease.

Acknowledgments

I had a seed. Rhoda Redleaf helped me plant it.

My editor, Beth Wallace, and my friend and colleague, Amy Gendall, made sure it sprouted.

Nourishment came from my respected colleagues at Northwest Interfaith Movement.

It was given room to grow by Richard R. Fernandez.

Early pruning was in the deft hands of Rick Eslinger, Ilene Silk, Denise Ellis, and Annette Freeman.

Final cuts were made masterfully by Beth Wallace.

It's yours for the taking.
Enjoy the harvest.

Special appreciation to

Harry O. Wilson and Terrie Watch for introducing me to theme kits.

Debbie Eastwood Ravaçon for opening the door to a special connection with the USA Toy Library Association, the group that continues to inspire me.

My special friend, Deena Webb Moss, and librarian extraordinaire, Holly Carlson—masters of children's literature.

Upper Dublin Township Public Library—they collected countless books for me, not knowing why, and never questioned my sanity.

Table of Contents

Introduction

Why this book? Why now? It's simple: I love planning with themes, and I think they deserve some renewed attention. I developed my passion for themes while teaching kindergarten at a community-based private school in Philadelphia. The school was located adjacent to the campus of the University of Pennsylvania, in an inner-city neighborhood serving a widely diverse group of children. The themes selected for our kindergarten curriculum gave us common ground. We all had something to offer and much to learn. I found myself fascinated by trucks, ships, and small city animals. For example, I discovered that if I stood on a pedestrian walking bridge and did a pulling motion (using a raised arm) to passing trucks, they would toot their horns. I became an expert on parts of a ship and fell in love with the power of tugboats.

The long-lasting impact of learning through themes is impressive, as is the amount of time that goes into this type of teaching. Not until I left the classroom, and had opportunities to reflect on this thematic approach, did I realize how incredibly time consuming it was to delve into themes so deeply. But if I hadn't committed tremendous time and energy to developing each theme, I would have risked losing the inherent value in teaching thematically. I was introduced to theme kits in my position as Resource and Training Coordinator with the Philadelphia Early Childhood Collaborative. The Collaborative has six resource rooms throughout the city that loan theme kits, educational toys, equipment, and resources to anyone engaged with young children. With theme kits the investment of time is up front, and the payoff is long-term. It's time for educators to take a close look at teaching with themes, agree on what makes them effective teaching tools, and discover how theme kits can make this approach practical as well!

Theme-based curriculum takes in a wide range of practice. Not all thematic teaching looks alike, nor should it. But certain elements need to be present for thematic teaching to be appropriate for young children. Let's look at what makes themes an effective teaching tool and what traps we need to look out for. After all, the goats in the classic children's story, "The Three Billy Goats Gruff," were willing to risk life and limb to get to greener pastures; we early childhood professionals could benefit from a harmless walk across a different bridge. The goats had exhausted the supply of nutrient-rich grass by staying in one place for too long; teachers are way too smart to let that happen. We know that the best education for children comes from constantly evaluating and changing our own behavior to keep the learning rich with fresh nutrients!

Effective theme-based teaching allows us to teach everything in the curriculum while adhering to developmentally appropriate practice (DAP). DAP is based on research about how children learn and develop. These principles of our profession are defined in the National Association for the Education of Young Children's (NAEYC) position statement, "Developmentally Appropriate Practice in Early Childhood Programs." Thematic teaching must be based on these principles to be effective. Theme kits are a means to move from theme teaching that has lost its grounding in these principles to teaching that depends on these ideals. The focus here is on understanding the benefits of good thematic teaching, and on developing and using theme kits to make those benefits a reality.

Themes supported by kits benefit children in a variety of ways:

- Children learn concepts through meaningful exploration over an extended period. Good theme topics encourage each child's involvement across all developmental domains. The learning of basic skills comes naturally from each child's physical, social, emotional, and cognitive engagement with materials and activities that are available for several weeks.

- Children have time to take hold of a concept and to integrate it into their existing knowledge. Themes encourage children to represent their new knowledge through art, dramatic play, building activities, and other areas of the curriculum. Through play, children deepen their understanding of new ideas.

- Children master concepts through repeated experiences with materials and activities. A broad range of experiences will capitalize on each child's preferred or dominant learning mode.

- Children have opportunities to reveal interests, talents, and innate abilities. (After a week of studying trucks, some children will be able to name and describe the differences between a dump truck, a cement truck, a tractor-trailer, and so on. Some will know which truck has four wheels and which has eighteen, which does construction work and which carries materials long distances, or how the movement of a cement truck keeps the cement at a workable consistency.) Math, science, language, and cognitive skills are being built before our eyes—we mustn't diminish the importance of this learning by ending the study of trucks before these concepts take hold.

Teachers and family child care providers also benefit from using themes:

- Classroom management becomes easier as children are *actively* engaged in meaningful work.

- Preparation for class time is lessened. Teachers present more open-ended materials, ending the need for precut materials and prepared worksheets.

- Work becomes more fulfilling and satisfying as children and teachers share excitement and commitment to interesting projects.
- Parents share in the enthusiasm for what children are learning and appreciate teachers in a new way.

Teaching with themes can provide all of these benefits for children and teachers. However, too often themes are used in ways that sabotage children's learning, and actually make work harder for teachers. Theme-based teaching that is not grounded in knowledge of child development doesn't result in real learning. Here are some signs of ineffective thematic curriculum:

- Children are expected to learn new concepts in a week's time and don't have opportunities to manipulate relevant materials. (Children need more time to develop interests and extrapolate meaning.)
- Thematic activities are limited so that not all learning styles are honored. There may be visual presentations, but nothing for children who learn best by auditory and tactile experiences.
- The teacher's goal is to finish the objectives by the end of a predetermined period, often a week; children do not have time to integrate their new learning.
- Children get introduced to concepts but don't have opportunities to apply them.
- Children have limited opportunities to practice their new knowledge and skills. This makes it hard for them to build confidence, and makes it less likely that they will retain what they've learned.
- Children do not have input into what topics to study and how to explore them. This makes it less likely that they will be interested in the theme. It is likely to be harder to hold their attention, and their learning is likely to be shallow.

Developing theme kits, as described in this book, will help teachers avoid the shortcomings of theme-based teaching, while capitalizing on the benefits of this popular approach. Theme kits contain a variety of developmentally appropriate materials and activities that relate to a specific topic, including books, audiocassettes, puzzles, open-ended materials, and play props. The materials appeal to different senses and learning styles (for example, a wild animal theme kit reinforces animal names through visual, auditory, and tactile modalities). They are carefully selected for cultural relevance and inclusion and to avoid bias.

The effectiveness of the materials depends on the relationship of the child and the teacher. A successful relationship comes from the teacher paying attention to the child's responses. If a child doesn't learn the names of farm animals by looking at pictures, the teacher can dig deeper into the theme kit or add something that works to the collection of materials. It may be the song, the puppets, or the small sorting animals that bring meaning to each animal and its name. For me, it probably would have been the cow-shaped cookies!

The purpose of this book is threefold: to share my passion for themes, to inspire creativity on the part of educators and young children in their use of themes, and to ensure that young children keep alive their sense of wonder and delight in learning new things. As author and lifelong teacher Mimi Brodsky Chenfeld (2000) says in response to her students' excitement over one child's play fire hat, "Be creative, be imaginative, be flexible, be open-minded, be playful, be holistic, be courageous, be tuned into kids, be brilliant, and figure out ways to link a fire to every other subject or topic. In other words, make connections!"

I hope that teachers who use this book will learn about themes that work well; where to find materials and resources; and how to develop, maintain, and use a theme kit most effectively. I hope the theme kit approach to curriculum keeps teachers and children stimulated by the process of learning. Children will learn language, math, and problem-solving skills and science and social studies concepts. They will develop socially, physically, and cognitively every step of the way.

A Note about Terms

Are we teachers, caregivers, early childhood educators, or baby-sitters? Well, we know what we are not! But it is harder to agree on language that suits all people who work directly with young children in a child care or preschool setting. A recent survey on preferred job titles of early childhood staff produced the following results. Home-based providers preferred "family child care provider," and staff in a larger group setting preferred "teacher" (Center for Early Childhood Leadership 2001). This book will use both terms where possible, and use the term "teacher" to apply to all readers where brevity is needed.

References

Center for Early Childhood Leadership. 2001. *Research Notes* (Summer).

Chenfeld, Mimi Brodsky. 2000. Get the elephant out of the room! We're finished with the E's! *Young Children* 55, no. 6: 21.

National Association for the Education of Young Children. 1996. Principles of child development and learning that inform developmentally appropriate practice. Position statement.

Chapter 1

Theme Kit Basics

A theme kit is a tool to support active, developmentally appropriate learning while honoring and celebrating different learning styles and strengths, individual interests, and each child's social and cultural contexts. Theme kits contain culturally sensitive educational materials, manipulatives, props, and resources for the purpose of teaching young children about an identified topic, or *theme*. The contents of a kit include all your great ideas, materials, play props, books, music, and recipes—in other words, the collections that once cluttered your home or classroom. A theme kit is like a concrete, three-dimensional lesson plan, and contains materials to support all areas of your curriculum.

Why Use Theme Kits?

To save time and aggravation

If you are a teacher or family child care provider and anything like me, you have pages of ideas, activities, finger plays, recipes, and more . . . everywhere. Congratulations if they are actually organized in a file of some sort. Even with all the ideas in one place, I found myself scrambling every time I started a new unit. The animal puppets were buried at the bottom of my daughter's toy box, the perfect books were at three different local libraries, and the bird's nest did not survive the year at the bottom of my storage closet. Organizing materials by theme saves time, energy, and aggravation.

To support best practice

Young children learn through exposure to a wide variety of materials and experiences that encourage exploration and discovery. A well-built kit includes the resources you need to support learning. Putting together a kit helps teachers think clearly ahead of time about the materials that will best support children's learning.

To increase school readiness

Thoughtful thematic planning encourages optimal development and readiness for the curriculum that awaits children in the elementary school setting (Bowman, Donovan, and Burns 2001). Educators of young children have the enviable opportunity to make lifelong learners of their students. Children come to us eager to discover, explore, and engage in meaningful interactions. When you develop a theme kit, you take the time to include items that support active, child-initiated learning.

To address staff turnover

If you are the director of a child care program, you know that consistency is essential. Yet you cannot control the revolving door of staff turnover. You can, however, influence programming in each class by providing the staff with a library of theme kits.

The theme kits will introduce a new teacher to the philosophy of your program better than your handbook or your shelf of curriculum guides. With theme kits, new staff can adopt an effective thematic approach easily. Over time, teachers will add their own ideas and materials to existing kits, and build new kits from their experiences and interests. Now you have a chance to enrich your program for the long run, even if employment is often short-term.

Selecting Themes

It is important to use your limited resources and unlimited creativity to choose your themes carefully. In Sylvia Chard's words, "Not all topics are equally promising in terms of their educational potential" (1998, 27). Consider the following factors when selecting themes for kits.

Ages of children

Young preschool children will respond better to more concrete topics that reflect their current experiences. There are always exceptions to this guideline—how else can we explain children's fascination with dinosaurs?

Availability of appropriate, bias-free materials

It would be exciting to study space, but it might be a challenge to find hands-on materials that reflect gender and racial diversity and are appropriate for young children.

Opportunities to make connections from topic to life experiences

Even if children have never seen a farm, they experience the products from a farm every day. Some connections might not be immediately obvious nor relevant for each child in the group, and that is okay. If no one is making connections, you will know soon enough by the blank, unresponsive faces of the children.

Opportunities for meaningful social interactions

Will a topic provide opportunities for dramatic play, teamwork, and peer support?

Connections to family and community

Will families be able to contribute culturally relevant materials and ideas for the study? Can members of the community or places in the community support the topic?

Level of intrigue

Magic vocabulary is a term coined by educator Mimi Chenfeld (2000, 20) to describe ideas that enthrall children. Children may have their own magic vocabularies, or there may be a class vocabulary. By tuning in, you can begin to capture these vocabularies and turn them into future theme kits. Your observations will clue you in. Use these questions to get you started:

As you observe the children at play, what ideas generate excitement?

As you listen to children converse, what are the consistent themes?

As you speak to families about their children's interests, what do you discover about passions?

What stories do children like to hear over and over?

Possible Themes

Here are some categories of themes to get you started. You, the children, and the families in your program will think of many more possibilities.

Fairy tales, folktales, and nursery rhymes

Search the library and the Internet for nonviolent, bias-free versions of these classics. If you choose to use a classic version, find ways to address misrepresentations and inappropriate behaviors of people and animals.

Favorite stories

Spend time in the children's library or favorite bookstore, or visit a book Web site. Find a book that captures your imagination.

Universal themes

Think about experiences shared worldwide, such as eating, sleeping, playing, and celebrating. I include the babies theme in this category, because it introduces worldwide human similarities and encourages appreciation of cultural differences.

Discovery themes

These topics, mostly science-based, enhance the children's understanding of the natural world.

Health and safety

Learn how to take care of yourself and others. The topics here are important for the entire family, not just the child. We cannot overemphasize the importance of nutrition, physical activity, fire prevention, and healthy lifestyles.

Toy Librarians Take Note
Traditional theme topics are in the greatest demand in my resource room. It is important to have a solid collection from this category. Due to increased demand on a seasonal basis, it is wise to have multiple kits of popular topics.

On the job

These topics give you an opportunity to capitalize on the skills and talents of adults involved in your program and in the community.

Traditional themes

Some of your most creative and imaginative kits can be developed from the most basic topics, such as transportation, the city, the farm, and so on. It is your job to bring to life the sights, sounds, textures, smells, and tastes related to these subjects.

Explorations

This category encourages you to do an in-depth study of man-made or natural materials. Consider seashells, rocks, seeds, shoes, or hats as subjects for study.

Holiday themes

I began teaching in the generation that started to question the place of Christmas trees in schools. Over time, it seems that more and more public school systems have adopted stringent guidelines on the teaching and celebrating of religious holidays. While trying to grasp the range of practices in use, I found a position paper by Jane Davis Stone, a candidate for a master's degree at Pacific Oaks College in Pasadena, California. In "A Jehovah's Witness Perspective on Holiday Curriculum" (1991), she relates the following anecdote.

In her final curriculum class, the teacher asked the students to work in small groups and develop theme calendars. They were to start by entering every holiday they could think of on a commercial calendar. There was a buzz of activity as everyone filled in spaces. They discovered that there are more than a hundred typically celebrated days. Then the teacher said to throw the list away and form another list of themes that had nothing to do with holidays.

Stone asserts that children's imagination, creativity, and sense of wonder gets shortchanged when programs pay too much attention to holiday celebration. She asks the reader to use that energy studying open-ended ideas and encouraging children's natural curiosities. Isn't there already enough commercial attention paid to holidays? She encourages teachers to leave their safety zone of a holiday-driven curriculum in favor of a curriculum that reflects the natural world around them. Trip-trap, trip-trap—yet another bridge to cross.

I think the most important goal is to raise our own consciousness about the seriousness of this topic. There are some excellent resources available for educators on the use of holidays in the early childhood curriculum: *Celebrate: The Anti-Bias Guide to Enjoying Holidays* (Bisson 1997); *The Anti-Bias Curriculum: Tools for Empowering Young Children* (Derman-Sparks 1989); and *Roots and Wings: Affirming Culture in Early Childhood Programs* (York 1991). (See the resource list at the end of this chapter for complete information.) The guidelines in these books will help you approach holidays in your program ethically. According to the National Association for the Education of Young Children, teachers must "respect the dignity of each family and its culture, language, customs, and beliefs" (NAEYC 1998, I, 2.3). Given that so many holidays have religious connections, it becomes the responsibility of the teacher to be aware, knowledgeable, and respectful of the religious beliefs of each family and to make the classroom a friendly place for all children and families.

Building Your Kit

Once your theme is selected, you're ready to take action. I suggest that you use the following list to plan a theme and to figure out what to put in the theme kit.

- Develop a theme tree
- Consider learning styles
- Appeal to all the senses
- Reflect on the learning environment and daily routine
- Include resource materials to encourage the user to explore further
- Make sure the materials reflect the full spectrum of diversity
- Include open-ended materials
- Make the kit a manageable size
- Select durable items
- Assess the safety and practicality of your choices

Develop a theme tree

The kits in this book include sample theme trees—brainstorming made visible. This is a method to help your ideas flow. Themes are about building connections, just like brain development is about building synapses. You'll be surprised at how many ideas come to you as you let your mind wander. In the beginning, every idea counts—this is not yet the time to analyze anything. Just write.

Start with a blank piece of paper; draw a trunk and some branches to help you get started. On the trunk of your tree, write the name of the theme you plan to study. Let the branches lead you to topics that are part of your theme or maybe only vaguely related to it. For example, if you start with sleep as a theme, one set of branches might include beds, pillows, quilts, and stuffed animals; another branch might include dreams, nightmares, and bedtime fears.

The theme tree generates ideas and questions that become the guts of your plans. As you write the topics, use a separate piece of paper to jot down ideas and materials that immediately come to mind. When you have developed a nice, full tree, step back and look it over. Think about how each topic, material, or activity idea fits with your program goals. Look for balance. If too many materials support cognitive goals, and none support social-emotional goals, add more branches to your tree, and lop some existing ones off if necessary. If there are not enough materials to support small groups or individual play, make modifications.

Consider learning styles

Howard Gardner's theory of multiple intelligences gives educators and parents eight ways to view intelligence, each one associated with a dominant learning style. Each type of intelligence has equal value. For a teacher's purposes, the most important part of his theory to keep in mind is that "we are not all the same; we do not all have the same kinds of minds; and education works most effectively if these differences are taken into account" (Gardner 1999, 91). Gardner identified eight types of intelligence: linguistic, logical-mathematical, bodily-kinesthetic, intrapersonal, interpersonal, naturalist, spatial, and musical. By using a multidisciplinary approach to teaching, you are honoring the multiple intelligences of the children in your care. When you offer a wide variety of materials and activities for exploration, each child will have equal opportunity to learn from the experience.

Review the learning styles associated with each intelligence in the box on page 8. As you convert ideas from the theme tree into things to put in your theme kit, keep these different learning styles in mind.

Which type of learner does this kit support?

On the next page is a list of intelligence types defined by Howard Gardner (1999, 91), further explained with applications to early childhood education by the Please Touch Museum® of Philadelphia.

Intelligence Types	Characteristics	Activities and Materials to Include in Each Kit
Linguistic	Has sensitivity to all forms of language, affinity for learning languages, and ability to use language effectively	Picture books, flannelboard story pieces, puppets, poems, blank books, story-starter theme-related pictures, writing, reading, creative dramatics, circle time discussion
Logical-Mathematical	Has the capacity to analyze problems logically, do scientific investigations, and solve math problems	Problem-solving puzzles and games; science materials for exploration and experimentation; pattern-based manipulatives such as beads, parquetry blocks, cooking activities; and sets of theme-related props
Spatial	Has the skills used by navigators and pilots to understand large, open spaces, and the refined skills of surgeons and artists to work in confined space	3-D projects such as woodworking, collages, and constructions; building materials such as Legos and other interconnecting units
Bodily-Kinesthetic	Can use any or all parts of the body to solve problems or create products	Dance music, instruments, and movement props such as scarves, hoops, and balls; props for acting out stories; tactile materials such as raised-dot dominoes
Musical	Has skills in performance, composition, and appreciation of music (Traditionally viewed as a talent, in Gardner's view it is a learning style.)	Instruments, music-based activities, introduction to different music styles and genres
Interpersonal	Works well with others through understanding of the human psyche, and processes information through peoples' gestures, expressions, and body movements	Opportunities to be social with peers, to work cooperatively; experiences outside of classroom, field trips; puppets for puppet shows; small-group craft projects such as murals or building projects; group field trips, with children partnered in small groups
Intrapersonal	Uses self-knowledge to strengthen self-esteem, self-understanding, and self-discipline	Independent activities; theme-based computer sites or software; puzzles and independent learning games (matching and sorting activities); art easel with open-ended art materials; headphones and story tapes
Naturalist	Has expertise in classifying and identifying species in his or her environment (This intelligence has been important in our evolutionary history.)	Collections of natural materials, outdoor experiences, access to natural surroundings, science discoveries

Appeal to all the senses

We may not know what each child's dominant intelligence type is, but we do know that all children learn through their senses. Be sure children have an opportunity to use different senses in exploring the materials. A book about snakes will describe the texture of a snake's skin and the process of shedding. Your kit should also include actual skin that has been shed by a reptile. Any pet store or nature center will gladly donate freshly shed snakeskins.

Reflect on the learning environment and daily routine

Your daily schedule and your environment will influence the types of materials in your kit. Include items that will enhance block play, dramatic play, the reading/writing/listening centers, and art experiences. Is there something special that could be used at circle time, at outdoor time, or during nap? Thinking about your special routines and play and work areas might stimulate some interesting ideas.

Include resource materials to encourage the user to explore further

The user might be the child, the educator, or the parent. I find it helpful to have a fact sheet handy on the different topics included in a theme kit. You'll find sample fact sheets in the theme kits in this book. I was able to do fact sheets with minimal effort thanks to the Internet. My favorite search engine is Google.com. When putting together a fact sheet, look for factual information that extends the learning from the theme. Be sure to look at more than one resource—you may uncover areas where experts disagree, which can become fruitful avenues for exploration.

Make sure the materials reflect the full spectrum of diversity

All kits can be enriched by the addition of pictures that relate to the topic. Pictures can be found in magazines, calendars, specialty journals, and catalogs. When people and cultures are represented in the pictures, choose inclusive and bias-free images. Refer to the the anti-bias checklists on pages 10–12. Be cautious of commercially made posters and display materials that do more to enforce stereotypes than to dispel them.

Anti-Bias Checklist for Books, Toys, and Materials

Books

	Yes	No
Are characters able to solve their own problems?	❏	❏
Do the characters' actions emphasize the importance of helping others?	❏	❏
Do the pictures or words put down people based on their culture, gender, ability, race, or age?	❏	❏
If there are several characters, is there a balance of active males and females?	❏	❏

Toys and Materials

	Yes	No
Does this item stereotype people by gender, race, ethnicity, or ability?	❏	❏
Does the packaging or marketing of the item show stereotypes or ethnic bias?	❏	❏
Does the item have a TV counterpart that promotes bias and/or violence, either directly or through hidden messages?	❏	❏
Is the item useful in several different situations and equally available for all children?	❏	❏
Does this item reflect the philosophy and goals of my family child care home (center or school)?	❏	❏
As a whole, do the toys and materials encourage cooperation and celebrate diversity?	❏	❏

From *Helping Children Love Themselves and Others,*
The Children's Foundation, Washington, D.C. Used by permission

Quick Ways to Analyze Children's Books for Racism and Sexism

Check the illustrations

Look for stereotypes. While you may not always find blatant stereotypes, look for variations that demean or ridicule characters because of their race, ethnicity, culture, home language, gender, disability, class, or family makeup.

Look for tokenism. If there are characters who are people of color, do they look just like whites except for being tinted or colored in?

Who's doing what? Do the illustrations depict people of color, people with disabilities, or women in leadership and action roles?

Check the story line

What is the standard for success? Is "making it" in the dominant white society projected as the only ideal? In friendships between white children and children of color, is it the child of color who does most of the understanding and forgiving?

How are problems presented, conceived, and resolved in the story? Are people of color and their cultures or languages considered to be "the problem"?

Are the achievements of girls and women based on their own initiative and intelligence? Would the story be believable if the sex roles were reversed?

Look at lifestyles

Are people of color and their setting depicted in such a way that they contrast unfavorably with white middle-class suburbia? If the illustrations and text attempt to depict another culture, do they go beyond oversimplifying and offer genuine insights into another lifestyle? Watch for the "quaint-natives-in-costume" syndrome.

From *Helping Children Love Themselves and Others,*
The Children's Foundation, Washington, D.C. Used by permission

Weigh the relationships between people

Do white males possess the power, take the leadership, and make the important decisions? How are family relationships depicted?

Note the heroes

People of color have the right to define their own heroes (of both sexes) based on their own concepts and struggles for justice. Ask this question: "Whose interest is a particular hero really serving?"

Consider the effects on a child's self-image

Are norms established that limit any child's aspirations and self-concept? Can children of color readily identify with at least one character, to a positive and constructive end?

Consider the author's or illustrator's background

What qualifies the author or illustrator to deal with the subject?

Check out the author's perspective

Read carefully to determine whether the author's perspective substantially weakens or strengthens the value of the work.

Watch for loaded words

A word is loaded when it has insulting overtones. Examples of loaded adjectives are "savage," "primitive," "lazy," and "backward." Look for sexist language and adjectives that exclude or ridicule women.

Look at the copyright date

Not until the early 1970s did the children's book world begin to even remotely reflect the realities of a multiracial society. Nonsexist books, with rare exceptions, were not published before 1973. A recent copyright date, of course, is no guarantee of a book's relevance or sensitivity.

From *Helping Children Love Themselves and Others,*
The Children's Foundation, Washington, D.C. Used by permission

Include open-ended materials

An open-ended material is one that can legitimately be used in a number of ways or that has no correct answer. Water, sand, blocks, and modeling dough are examples of open-ended materials. Puzzles and worksheets that have one right answer are considered "closed." Both closed and open-ended materials are appropriate to include in theme kits, although of course such materials as water and sand may not be practical to include! However, it may take more effort to think of open-ended materials, particularly if you are unfamiliar with them.

Think about including open-ended items such as scarves, puppets, books, and building toys that can be used in a variety of creative ways. Generic open-ended materials that lend themselves to many themes should *not* be contained with each kit, but should be available to supplement work and play.

Make the kit a manageable size

My experience has been that it's worth identifying the basic components of a kit before you commit to a container. Consider, too, the long-term storage area available for finished kits. Most of the kits described in this book will fit in 18-gallon storage containers. You might decide to focus your energy on shoebox-size mini-kits that can be used in a home environment or smaller classroom setting.

Try to avoid the trap of using this container to collect every trinket, toy, book, and prop that relates to the theme. One of my many favorite children's books is *The Moon Came Too,* by Nancy White Carlstrom. A little girl fills a "bottomless" suitcase with all her favorite toys and special items for an overnight at Grandma's. She takes no chances; nothing is left behind. This approach may not serve you well in kit building. Be choosy. Think about how the material might be used to enhance the play and learning experience. Don't be afraid to take something out if it doesn't work.

Select durable items

Remember, you are *building* a kit. This is a process that relies on strong foundation materials that will support the final structure. If you want your kit to last over time, use durable supplies. Be a picky consumer. Beware of commercial products that match your theme but do not promote your goals. For example, when you talk about animals, you want children to learn to appreciate and recognize their physical characteristics and natural habitats. Do not use a set of animals that includes pink pandas and polka-dotted giraffes!

Frequently Asked Theme Kit Questions

If all my cool supplies—favorite books, puppets, games, and dramatic props—are in kits, what is left to be displayed in the room when I'm not using a theme kit?

Not to worry—lest you forget, teachers are pack rats by nature. You have more stuff than you'll ever know what to do with. Your room will always have the basic building toys, manipulatives, art materials, assortment of books, and puzzles.

Does the theme tree get packed up with the theme kit?

No. The theme tree existed for a particular purpose at a particular time. Next time you decide to do that theme, brainstorm a new list. Some new connections might have occurred to you since you last thought about this topic.

The thought of putting together theme kits exhausts me. Is there another way?

You can enlist creative and energetic parents, student teachers, or volunteers. For example, the staff at one of our resource rooms was approached by a women's auxiliary group that developed art appreciation kits for our school-age programs.

How can we find the funds to build a kit with quality books and materials?

Think strategically. Approach small funders who have specific interest areas. We received a grant to do an educational art project. We hired three artists to do workshops with children and teachers, and the culminating project was the production of three kits: clay, weaving, and silk screening. Each kit has a video of an artist showing the craft and contains all the tools necessary for children to work in that medium. There is a food co-op in our neighborhood that offers small grants to do recycling projects. We received a grant to develop three recycling kits, one for each age group. You're limited only by your imagination, not by your pocketbook.

Enjoy the process. Building a theme kit can be like shopping for a gift. You can enjoy the hunt and find the perfect gift, or pick the first thing you see within your budget. It's up to you how much time and energy you devote to this project. Remember that kits have beginnings, but no endings.

Assess the safety and practicality of your choices

There is one more set of considerations you must make before you begin to gather materials. Are your choices safe and practical? Use the following checklist to guide you.

❏ **If children under three will have access to materials, is a choke tube included?**
If you do not have a commercial choke tube, a film canister will suffice. Any item that fits completely within the canister is a choking hazard.

❏ **Are the items in the kit sturdy, and can you repair them if needed?**
If you're not handy, think twice before including materials that might need tweaking to stay operational.

❏ **Are the materials washable?**
My standard is if it can survive the washing machine, it makes the cut. Some of my puppets might look a bit raggedy after the spin cycle, but that's okay.

❏ **Are replacement parts available for commercial products?**
Some companies will replace lost parts. Do not include anything you consider valuable and irreplaceable.

❏ **Have you included multiples of items you expect to be popular?**
There will be other opportunities to teach sharing!

Acquiring Your Kit Contents

Finding materials for a theme kit is a long-range project. Think about what you want the children to gain from the experience. If you want children to learn about farms, you need more than a complete set of plastic farm animals. Seek and you shall find: unprocessed wool (feel the lanolin); a dried stem from a cotton plant; and hay, which is not just for horses! These items will not be at your local educational supply store. For my farm kit, I got wool from a local weaver, a cotton plant from a roadside stand, and hay at a pumpkin farm. For more basic needs, try these sources.

Catalog companies

Educational catalogs abound. See appendix 2 for a list of the ones I've found most helpful. Next time you go to a national or regional conference, collect catalogs from vendors. Think more broadly than early childhood catalogs. For example, library catalogs offer a broad selection of story-telling props, health care catalogs have medical props, and veterinary catalogs have pet props. We have an advantage over those who came before us—the Internet! Seek novel offerings such as Lehman's Non-electric Catalog (see appendix 2), the perfect source to acquire a grain mill as a prop for the story of The Little Red Hen.

Thrift stores

Don't be fooled by outside appearances; you'll find many treasures here. Thrift stores are especially useful for dress-up accessories and replacement parts. You are likely to find pieces to match missing parts of commercial materials.

Dollar stores

Dollar stores are taking over the discount shopping market. Here's where you'll find basters for the Water Kit, small hand tools for the Fix-it Shop Kit, and containers galore for sorting materials in any kit.

Garage or yard sales

You have to be a true bargain hunter at heart to enjoy this activity. It involves getting up early on Saturday morning and mapping out your route from the classifieds in your local papers. If you don't fancy the selection in your local neighborhood or would rather go unrecognized (good idea if you look like me early Saturday mornings), venture out to a more distant neighborhood. Look for theme-related puzzles, books, and play props. One time I happened upon a costume designer's yard sale. Imagine the possibilities!

Web sites

If you prefer to let your fingers do the walking, try doing online searches of theme topics. When I did a search for "Cinderella," the search engine found 221,019 documents in 0.741 seconds. In the first few pages of entries, I found some very useful sites. Appendix 2 has a list of Web sites I've found helpful.

Craft stores

Many craft stores have large selections of rubber stamps to accessorize your themes. The images should be realistic, no cutesy animals. Also, look for novelty items such as silk flowers and a wicker basket for Little Red Riding Hood. Craft stores sell containers with multiple compartments that may be useful for small items in your kit.

Bookstores and libraries

Some public library systems sell their used books. In Philadelphia, there is a book bank loaded with free library books that have been removed from circulation. I find that books are the backbone of most kits. Unfortunately, they are also the back breakers. Don't be afraid to begin with a few good books, and add others over the years.

Journals and magazines

This is one source of relevant background information for parents and staff. For example, the May 2001 issue of *Young Children* featured an article by Ann Epstein titled "Thinking about Art: Encouraging Art Appreciation in Early Childhood Settings." This would be perfect for an art appreciation kit. You will also be able to supplement kits with pictures and articles from magazines such as *Ranger Rick* and *Your Big Backyard* from the National Wildlife Federation.

Museum gift shops

Most museums will let you visit the gift shop without paying admission. At a science museum, you might find goodies like freeze-dried food, models of space ships, and toys that teach principles of gravity for a space kit. At a historical museum, look for high-quality handcrafted toys. Art museum shops and catalogs have some of the best materials for children. The education departments at museums can be a great resource. Also, get on the mailing list of museums that are not in your area. Patiently wait for seasonal sales to build your collections.

Vendors at conferences

I have found some of my favorite materials at the National Association for the Education of Young Children (NAEYC) conference vendor displays. Who would have thought there was a picture-book version of Little Red Riding Hood with a female woodcutter?

Additional resources

Primary caretakers of the children are your best resources. Be sure to include them in all your planning. Distribute lists of all the kits you are developing. Note the types of items needed to enrich each kit. Request that donations be submitted with the following information:

Name of item

Name of donor

Do you want this item back?   When?

If this item is on loan, is it replaceable if broken or damaged?

Is there any other information you'd like to share?

Storage Solutions

How in the world will you store all these acquisitions? If you need the kits to be portable, you have a whole other set of challenges. I've marked containers that would be especially useful for portability with the icon you see in the margin here. If the thought of adding more stuff to your nonexistent storage area has you ready to close this book, read on. Creative solutions are at your fingertips. Have you heard of a baby-sitting co-op? Try a theme kit co-op: rotate kits between family child care programs or classrooms. You could each store a couple of theme kits and they could be traded as needed. Who needs the extra calories of a cookie exchange when you could have a kit exchange and the time saved could be spent at the gym!

Plastic containers

There is a wide variety of plastic containers with lids and handles available commercially. Always wait for sales. Consider a box larger than the original contents so you have room to expand over time. Clear containers are more user-friendly, but tend to be less hardy. If the boxes are going to be transported, go for the sturdier versus the more attractive, transparent container. Office supply stores have a variety of file storage boxes, which are conveniently sized and portable. Plastic file boxes with handles are handy.

Pizza carriers

Make friends with your local pizza parlor and see if you can purchase the flat bags they use for deliveries from them. They stack well, and they can hold flat, large items such as puzzles and games. Similar bags can be purchased from specialized mail-order catalogs (see Charnstrom Mail Center Solutions in appendix 2).

Cloth bags

Modified versions of the theme kits presented in this book can be stored in mesh laundry bags. Washable mesh bags, ideal for toy storage, are available from the USA Toy Library Association (see appendix 2) in three different sizes. Bags with drawstrings can be hung from hooks so as not to take up any floor or shelf space. Visit the housewares aisle of your favorite discount store; if a bag can hold dirty laundry, it can hold educational materials. The new variety of pop-up bags, as small as 1-gallon size, have interesting possibilities. Shoemakers can work wonders with a vinyl or cloth bag that is missing one or more critical feature. Zippers, sturdy handles, and other accoutrements can be added.

Shopping bags

Discount and specialty stores use large carryall bags to assist customers with their shopping. Ask the retailer if bags could be donated or sold at discount; after all, you're offering free advertising. (Kohl's and IKEA are two chains to try.)

Luggage on wheels

Lucky for us, the luggage industry has revolutionized its designs. Look for anything from duffel bags to full-size suitcases on wheels. Heavier kits will get more use if they can be mobile.

Luggage carts

These serve an important purpose for the toy library or resource center that loans kits. The heavy kits in large plastic totes can be transported on a cart.

Resealable plastic bags

Plastic storage bags are an invaluable organizational tool for items inside each kit. Keep a variety of sizes on hand. The 2-gallon size is hard to find, but worth the search! The freezer storage bags are the sturdiest and worth the added expense.

Manila envelopes

Run large manila envelopes or pocket folders (take off metal clasps and staples) through a laminator. Use a razor to reopen seals. Velcro pieces with adhesive can be used to reseal. Use for storing informational materials inside a kit.

Three-ring binders

A binder filled with plastic sleeves is another way to store supplemental information. Extra plastic sleeves allow new information to be added easily.

Tips for Kit Maintenance

Whether you are the sole owner and user of your kits or you will be loaning them, it is important to keep these suggestions in mind.

Make an inventory

This is an investment of time up front with long-lasting dividends. Enclose a checklist of all the items within. If you are loaning kits to outside borrowers, instruct each user to be sure all items are included as listed. The user will ultimately be responsible for missing items. A checklist will also be extremely valuable to the teacher who wants to be able to retrieve all the kit contents at the end of the unit. The list should include any information you will need to replace a lost or broken item.

Toy Librarians Take Note
If you will be loaning kits and plan to charge for loss or damage, include original prices and place of purchase.

Label every item for easy recovery

This is labor intensive, but useful. We rarely give up on a lost item. They do turn up at the strangest times and the most unique places! Develop a code that identifies the name of your program, and the specific kit that the item is from. For puzzles and game parts, code each piece. (Try Sharpie-brand permanent markers; use etching tools for hard-to-mark items.)

Keep file copies of all paper items

This makes it easy to replace forms and reference materials that aren't returned with the kit.

Resources

Bisson, Julie. 1997. *Celebrate: An anti-bias guide to enjoying holidays.* St. Paul: Redleaf Press.

Bowman, Barbara M., Suzanne Donovan, and M. Susan Burns, eds. 2001. *Eager to learn: Educating our preschoolers.* Washington, D.C.: National Academy Press.

Bredekamp, Sue, and Carol Copple, eds. 1997. *Developmentally appropriate practice in early childhood programs.* Washington, D.C.: National Association for the Education of Young Children.

Chard, Sylvia C. 1998. *The project approach: Developing the basic framework.* New York: Scholastic Inc.

Chenfeld, Mimi Brodsky. 2000. Get the elephant out of the room! We're finished with the E's! *Young Children* 55, no. 6: 20.

Derman-Sparks, Louise. 1989. *The anti-bias curriculum: Tools for empowering young children.* Washington, D.C.: National Association for the Education of Young Children.

Epstein, Ann S. 2001. Thinking about art: Encouraging art appreciation in early childhood settings. *Young Children* 56, no. 3: 38–43.

Gardner, Howard. 1999. *Intelligence reframed: Multiple intelligences for the 21st century.* New York: Basic Books.

McCracken, Janet Brown, ed. 1990. *Helping children love themselves and others: A professional handbook for family day care.* Washington, D.C.: The Children's Foundation.

National Association for the Education of Young Children (NAEYC). 1997. Principles of child development and learning that inform developmentally appropriate practice. NAEYC position statement. www.naeyc.org/resources/position_statements/dap3.htm.

National Association for the Education of Young Children and International Reading Association. 1998. Code of ethical conduct and statement of commitment. Brochure. Washington, D.C.: NAEYC.

Please Touch Museum®. Which doors lead to learning? Online workshop. pleasetouchmuseum.com

Stone, Jane Davis. 1991. A Jehovah's Witness perspective on holiday curriculum. Unpublished position paper, Pacific Oaks College, Pasadena, Calif.

York, Stacey L. 1991. *Roots and wings: Affirming culture in early childhood programs.* St. Paul: Redleaf Press.

Toy Librarians Take Note
Make a list of "Additional Items You Might Want to Supply" addressed to the borrower. Costly, fragile, or consumable items such as a camera, batteries, or art materials might be included on this list. Consider loaning an instant or digital camera as a separate item. Consider asking for usage fees or a deposit.

Chapter 2

Theme Kits in Use

Your ideas are flowing, you've spent your budget allowance, and your attic is empty—you have put your first kit together. Great! Now, once it's all in the box, how do you bring it back out? The key to effective theme-based teaching is knowing how to use this wealth of materials while keeping the best interest of each child in mind. This chapter describes how to use the kits effectively in your home or classroom. To adapt them to the needs of your own program, keep the following general procedure in mind.

1. Set the tone; you are about to welcome the children into a world of new ideas. Gather the children around the closed box. Reveal the name of the theme. What does it make them think of? What do they think might be inside the box? This is a mystery about to unfold.

2. Pick out something that will pique their interest. It might be an artifact, a story, or a puppet that has a tale to tell. Bring out the rest of the materials a little at a time, over a few days.

3. Begin investigating the theme with the children. Ask the children what they already know about the topic. If they have mistaken ideas, make a note to supply experiences that will help children expand their knowledge. Learn about the children's experiences with the topic.

For example, if your theme is Little Red Riding Hood, talk about grandparents and learn the word in the home language of each child. Do they have a *zeydah,* a *pop-pop,* an *abuela,* or a *nanna?*

4. Record questions and comments that arise as children listen to stories and explore materials for the first time. What do they want to know more about? Stay tuned to children's questions and areas of interest; take cues from the children on how to develop your theme. Based on their responses, you can choose to expand or reduce your topic. If the theme is sea life and the children only want to talk about sharks, then sharks get main stage! By the end of the unit, you may be well on your way to having a second kit on sharks. Throughout the unit, encourage children to reflect, predict, question, and hypothesize.

5. As you bring materials out, discuss with the children where they think the materials should be placed in the room. For example, don't assume books only belong in the reading area. Encourage the children to think outside the box. Are there nonfiction books that might work well in the science or block-building area? Is there a special place for materials that need to be handled with extra care?

6. Look for signs of enthusiasm. Add materials and activities to the unit to build upon interests. Explore options for visitors and trips to complement the unit.

7. Get families involved from the start. Welcome them to see the contents of the kit and contribute ideas to enrich it. Remember the theme tree described in chapter 1? Instead of filling it in yourself, you could try inviting children and families to develop the theme. Hang a blank tree in an accessible place, with the theme name written on the trunk. Explain to the children and families that the branches need to be filled in with their ideas about the main topic. The only rule is that all ideas are welcome. This tree can grow as your project grows. From the tree, lessons and activities sprout, and you may come up with new materials to add to the kit.

8. Assess the children's learning. If you provide developmentally appropriate activities in a nurturing and supportive environment, children will learn. You will have to observe carefully in order to know what they are learning and to be able to document their learning, however. For example, you may observe children using new concepts in their play and conversation. This will tell you that meaningful learning is taking place. By providing opportunities for children to express themselves through a variety of media such as paint, building materials, drawing tools, and imaginative props, you will begin to see symbolic representation of their new knowledge. These representations can be displayed in photographs of children's work and placed on or near your original planning tree.

When children look at photo images of their play, activities, and projects, they revisit their learning and new questions emerge. Finally, help children reflect on the outcomes of their activities. Consider reflection as part of the learning experience as you assess what knowledge the child has gained.

9. Relax when week one draws to a close. Your children have already started to plan for week two, expanding on their early experiences.

The Classroom Environment

Your children are primed and ready; now it's time to focus on your space. Is your room setup conducive to teaching with theme kits? You might find a book like *The Creative Curriculum for Early Childhood* (Dodge and Colker 1995) or *The Creative Curriculum for Family Child Care* (Dodge and Colker 1991) useful for step-by-step setup of an optimal learning environment, based on developmental knowledge. An environment that fosters creativity for educators and children will naturally develop each person's interests and strengths.

Let the contents of the theme kit infiltrate existing interest areas or ones you plan to develop. Change your environment for each theme. If I were to visit your home or program today, would I be able to tell from clues in the environment what topic the children are exploring?

Each kit description in the following chapters will illustrate some ways to filter the theme across the curriculum and into different interest areas. Of course, the best ideas will come from you and the children.

Daily routines

Don't forget to work your theme into daily routines, as well as special events. Some ideas will lend themselves to materials and resources for your kit; some might happen more spontaneously and won't result in materials for the permanent kit collection.

Arrival

Vary your welcome routine to set the tone for your theme. Is there a cow puppet welcoming each child to the farm, or a ticket collector to board the train?

Breakfast

Look for ways to bring your theme to breakfast. If your site has a food program, you might not be able to vary menu choices. Try including theme-connected placemats and centerpieces in your kits.

Circle

Introduce a new item from the kit each day.

Free play

Each theme kit will have materials to add to your learning and play centers.

Outdoor play

Invent ways to bring your theme to your outdoor "rooms." For example, items in your kit can be used for theme-related treasure hunts.

Small group

This is the time to introduce some of the materials and learning games from the kit to a few children at a time. Use small group time to put on puppet shows, work on projects, and explore new materials.

Lunch

As with breakfast, try special placemats, creative menus, decorative centerpieces, and background music.

Rest time

Play a story tape, related nature tapes, or music you haven't played before. Make sure your selection includes different musical genres and reflects a wide variety of cultures.

Interest areas

Blocks and building

You'll be surprised to see the influence themes have on construction! Illustrations in fairy tales might lead to the building of castles, moats, and secret chambers. The addition of novel materials such as royal play people, new scenery, and a set of horses will entice new children to the block area. Keep paper and crayons or markers in the block area so children can make signs to warn visitors of "Danger" and "Projects under Construction."

Dramatic play

In many programs, the house area is converted to a dramatic play area to support different themes. However, you never know what family or household event children will need to play out in a house setting. Discuss this with the children in your program. Do they like the idea of the house becoming a supermarket for a month? Would they like you to find another corner in the room where they would still have access to baby dolls and basic household props?

If you have the luxury of space, maintain a dramatic play area separate from the house area. This will change according to the unit of study. Each kit will include suggested signs to post around the play areas. You or the children can make these signs. Tuning children in to the printed word is an early step towards reading. Children will come to look forward to new signs being posted in the play areas as you introduce new themes.

Math and manipulative center

The National Council of Teachers of Mathematics (NCTM) has established principles and standards outlining mathematics goals for prekindergarten through grade 12. The same ten principles apply to all grade levels. The standards are explained in detail at the NCTM standards Web site (standards.nctm.org).

The early childhood standards cover prekindergarten through grade 2 and can be somewhat intimidating to the preschool teacher. However, you'll find that mathematics is already a natural part of your day-to-day work with children in preschool settings. Math goals for preschoolers include understanding numbers and relationships (not just being able to count by rote); developing one-to-one correspondence; sorting items by categories (all the blue buttons, or all those with four holes); sequencing items (for example, from biggest to smallest); creating, reproducing, and comparing patterns; developing interest in shapes and measurement; and making predictions based on observations. Children should be able to develop these and other mathematical skills by playing in all the different learning centers, not just in the math and manipulative area. If you are providing a stimulating environment that encourages active engagement with materials, you can feel confident that the children are establishing a foundation for more complex concepts to come.

Suggestions for materials to supplement your math and manipulative area are included in the Ready, Set, Go section of each theme kit. This is your chance to replace the colored teddy bear counters with items from the theme kit that connect to the children's interests.

Art and projects

"Instead of racking your brain thinking of cute things for children to make to take home, rack your brain thinking of interesting materials for children to use" (Miller 1997, 36). Art is very different from crafts and projects. This is a place for children to express themselves through open-ended materials, including paint, modeling clay, and collage materials.

In many cases, this section of each theme kit will suggest project ideas. Projects serve very different purposes than art experiences. Projects reinforce concept ideas, build vocabulary, and teach listening skills. Don't let projects get in the way of the availability of open-ended art materials. If children choose to paint a theme-related picture at the easel, so be it. If their work is not related to the theme, take that as a clue to what interests them right now, and build on what you see. Children might choose open-ended materials related to the theme, or they might not. That's the beauty of open-ended materials.

Sensory station

Themes present opportunities to alter the experience of sand and water play. New materials can be added to simulate a different environment. Learning about polar bears? Fill the water table with ice. Want to know how a pig feels rolling around in mud? Prepare a mixture of dirt and water. Theme kits contain tools to explore new sensory materials. It might be a balance scale to weigh rocks, a grain mill to grind wheat, or other supplemental tools.

Book corner

Even public libraries have much more than books in the children's department. Consider adding a fish tank, photo albums, and a listening center to your book corner. Thematic puzzles have just as much of a place here as books. What in your kit would be a welcome addition to the book area?

New discoveries

I avoid calling this a science area because the word "science" paralyzes so many early childhood teachers. But when you really think about it, it's hard to think of something that is not science related! Science is about observing, identifying, describing, and investigating matter and events. It includes biology, the study of all living organisms; geology, the study of the earth; chemistry, the study of matter; and much, much more.

The problem with the science areas I see in classrooms is that once the children are there, it's not clear what they can or should do. Let children know that making observations is important work. Provide a tape recorder to encourage oral observations; provide journals, paper, and writing and drawing tools for written or dictated observations.

Writing center

A writing center is a place for children to come when they want to express their thoughts in print. If you're daring, keep a service bell at the writing table, so that a child who needs assistance with dictation can alert an adult.

Always have special paper at the writing center for children who want to make their own signs to support the theme. For example, they might make signs that lead Little Red Riding Hood to grandmother's house.

Music and movement area

It's funny how we early educators spend so much time thinking of art activities to include in our plans each week; when did art take on more significance than music in our society? Janice Beaty, author of *Preschool Appropriate Practices,* says children should have the "time to get as deeply involved with music as they do with blocks and books and paints" (Beaty 1992, 195).

Music sets the mood for many themes, and each kit should have cassettes or compact discs included as well as props for movement activities. Set up a work station for children to make simple instruments.

Family involvement

I once worked in a nursery school cooperative where family members were assigned to assist in the classroom a few times a year, do classroom and outdoor maintenance work, and participate on the board of directors or in committees. Head Start families are often similarly expected to be present in the classroom on a routine basis. But this level of family participation is unusual in child care programs today. Most adults are busy at work or in school themselves and are not available during the preschool day. It is incumbent on teachers and family child care providers to find creative ways to involve the families in the child's early education. Here are some possibilities:

Survey families

Develop a questionnaire for each family. Remember you're not just enrolling a child in your program, you're enrolling a whole family. The more you know about each person, the more successful each relationship will be. The questionnaire can be written or oral, whichever method makes everyone feel most comfortable. All questions are optional:

What is your work or school schedule?

What kind of work do you do? If you are a student, what are you studying?

Some of the theme kits we have planned for the year are (list kits). Do you have any interests, information, resources, or items that relate to these topics?

Sometimes we develop theme kits based on the interests of the children and families in our program. Do you have any ideas for us?

You are welcome to participate in our program at any time. If you are not able to visit our class, what is the best way for us to keep you informed about our activities? Would you prefer a newsletter, a daily note, or activities to be sent home?

Are you more likely to have a few extra minutes to chat at the beginning of the day, or at the end of the day?

Sometimes we might ask you to send something to help us learn about a theme. The requests shouldn't require you to do special shopping. Is two days enough notice for these requests?

Request feedback

Parent feedback is essential to the success of your theme. You'll want to know what the children are talking about or representing in their play at home. Do yourself and the children a special favor and guide the families on how to acquire information at the end of the day. "What did you do today?" is the most common question parents ask children. "Nothing," is the most common answer. By illustrating some pointers for parents, you will be saving your reputation and protecting the children from badgering.

The more a family member knows about the events of the day, the more successful their conversations with their children will be. Encourage family members to use conversation starters such as, "I saw that your dramatic play area was set up like a beach today. What was at your beach?" "What could we do at home to pretend we're at the beach?" "Who did you play with today?" "Who did you sit next to at circle time?"

Help parents understand what their children are learning

"A theme is fun for play, but what does my child learn each day?" I know in my heart, and, thanks to ongoing research, we all know in our brains that the best thing we can do with young children is let them be young children. As noted early childhood author and pediatrician Dr. T. Berry Brazelton has written, "Hurrying the child through any stage can actually slow him down. The cost is great. A shaky foundation is then built, just as hurrying up the foundation of a house may leave it vulnerable to the first hurricane" (Brazelton and Greenspan 2000, 116). Most early childhood teachers also know all the important learning that takes place while children are "just playing." However, many parents are legitimately concerned about their children's academic learning, and they want to be sure that they are providing the best possible learning opportunities for their children. It's not easy for them to see the solid foundation of skills, information, and concepts that children develop in a play-based curriculum.

There is national interest in the concept of school readiness. In some ways, this focus heightens the already high anxiety level of parents concerned about their children succeeding. You must be the voice of reason, helping parents understand how their child is developing, what they are learning through the thematic curriculum, and why it would actually be harmful to the children to expect their learning to look like the more academic learning of a first- or third-grader.

Use the information below as a guide to start a dialogue with parents concerned about academic achievements. This chart shows the components of each theme kit in this book, and the learning you can expect to see in children when you use each element. You can help parents understand that "Development occurs in a relatively orderly sequence, with later abilities, skills, and knowledge building on those already acquired" (NAEYC 1997, 10). Asking a three-year-old to learn to sit still and quiet for long periods of time, "to prepare them for a traditional primary grade classroom," is as ludicrous as asking a middle-aged person to practice sitting in a rocking chair for long periods of time to prepare for their later years. It is your role to assure parents that your goals are clear and your activities are appropriate. The themes in this book have been carefully designed to support cognitive, language, reading, writing, math, physical, social, and emotional development.

Kit Contents, Learning Experiences and Outcomes

Each kit in this book contains the following elements. Your kits may have different components, but you can use this list as a guide to thinking about the learning your kits support. Learning experiences are what the child does with the materials and activities. Learning outcomes are the desired results or consequences from the experiences.

- **Poem**

  Learning experiences: Hearing the poem read out loud; listening for the words that sound alike; making up new verses to the poem

  Learning outcomes: Children learn new vocabulary; develop phonological awareness; listen for content without visual cues; predict rhymes; develop other rhymes; conjure up visual images from auditory language. These are all pre-reading skills.

- **Books**
  Learning experiences: Hearing books read aloud; reading books to self and others; comparing different versions of the same story or different representations of the same character; researching information in non-fiction books

  Learning outcomes: Children sequence events from stories; connect images, print, and oral language; take pleasure in stories, which stimulates their desire to read; use critical thinking skills; solve problems; add to their existing knowledge and integrate new knowledge on a topic; use books as resources.

- **Commercial and teacher-made learning manipulatives, games, and collections**
  Learning experiences: Putting together puzzles; playing games; building, patterning, sorting, and sequencing with manipulatives and collections

  Learning outcomes: Children become adept at important pre-math and pre-reading skills such as matching, sorting, counting, sequencing, and patterning; children practice social skills such as turn-taking and working together to solve a problem or reach a goal.

- **Props**
  Learning experiences: Engaging in dramatic play with props connected to the theme; retelling stories and creating new ones using flannelboards or puppets

  Learning outcomes: Children learn the function of common household tools using trial and error; develop innovation and confidence by using props in imaginative ways; learn sequencing through retelling stories; experiment with language; practice new vocabulary and integrate new concepts; learn important social skills such as collaboration and negotiation.

- **Signs**
  Learning experience: Posting preprinted signs with meaning to them; making signs; reading signs that others have posted

  Learning outcomes: Children learn that the printed word has meaning; begin to recognize initial letter sounds; begin to understand that a word is a unit; may begin to print letters and compose words using invented spelling.

- **Other materials**
  Learning experiences: Seeing, feeling, and using everyday items from various cultures

Learning outcomes: Children speculate and hypothesize about how a particular item is used; become comfortable with seeing things done in new and unfamiliar ways.

- **Family involvement**

  Learning experiences: Composing letters to parents and preparing work for exhibit; documenting investigation of the theme and sharing experiences and thinking with families; using families as resources for further information and study

  Learning outcomes: Children build self-esteem; develop pride in own cultural heritage; consolidate knowledge through explanation and discussion.

Learning in the interest areas

Children's pre-academic learning is supported not only by the special items in a theme kit, but also by play in the interest areas in the classroom, which may or may not be modified as part of a theme. Here's a brief list of basic interest areas and the skills children develop as they play; for a more complete list, see *The Creative Curriculum, 3rd Edition.*

- **Blocks and building**

  Social/emotional skills—Learn to cooperate and be part of a team

  Cognitive skills—Observe cause and effect, make predictions

  Mathematical skills—Learn uses of geometry, fractions, and measurement

- **Dramatic play**

  Social/emotional skills—Try out various roles, solve problems in social situations, share props

  Language skills—Practice conversational language while acting roles, shop for food

  Mathematical skills—Use one-to-one correspondence

- **Art and projects**

  Physical skills—Use large and small muscles to manipulate art tools

  Creative skills—Develop multiple means of self-expression; construct knowledge about the theme concepts using artistic media

  Cognitive skills—Learn about colors, shapes, sizes, descriptive language

- **Sensory station**

  Physical skills—Use all senses to hypothesize and draw conclusions; heighten sensitivity

- **New discoveries**
  Cognitive skills—Observe, explore, predict, draw conclusions

- **Writing center**
  Pre-reading and writing skills—Practice sequencing, sorting, patterning, letter formation, stringing letters together, following and creating increasingly complex story lines

- **Music and movement**
  Physical skills—Develop sense of rhythm, purpose in movement
  Cognitive skills—Become aware of different types of music

Resources

Beaty, Janice J. 1992. *Preschool appropriate practices.* 2d ed. Fort Worth, Tex.: Harcourt Brace College Publishers.

Brazelton, T. Berry, and Stanley I. Greenspan. 2000. *The irreducible needs of children.* Cambridge: Perseus Publishing.

Bredekamp, Sue, and Carol Copple, eds. 1997. *Developmentally appropriate practice in early childhood programs.* Revised edition. Washington, D.C.: NAEYC.

Dodge, Diane Trister, and Laura J. Colker. 1991. *The creative curriculum for family child care.* Washington, D.C.: Teaching Strategies, Inc.

———. 1995. *The creative curriculum for early childhood.* 3d ed. Washington, D.C.: Teaching Strategies, Inc.

Miller, Karen. 1997. Creative activities for infants and toddlers. *Child Care Information Exchange* (January): 36.

National Council of Teachers of Mathematics (NCTM). 2000. *Principles and standards for school mathematics.* Reston, Va.: NCTM.

Vogel, Nancy. 2001. *Making the most of plan-do-review: Teacher's idea book 5.* Ypsilanti, Mich.: High/Scope Foundation.

Chapter 3

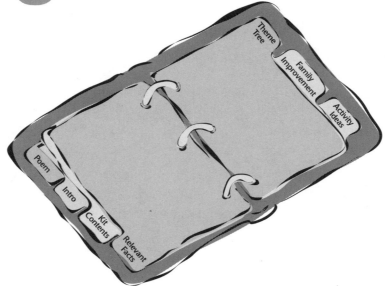

Theme Kit Guidelines

The themes and activities included in this book are most appropriate for children from three to six years old. The ideas are suggestions only. Like a book of story starters, this book is full of theme starters. You and the children will be the true creators of your theme kits.

Theme Kit Elements

Each theme kit description includes the following elements. You will probably want to include some of the written material with the kit. I use a three-ring binder with plastic sleeves to organize all the written material.

Poem

Why include poems at the beginning of each theme? Because I love poems in the classroom. Children get so much out of hearing rhyming sounds. A poem engages the interest of the children when you begin a new theme. Read the poem to the children at large group time to whet their appetites for the topic. Read it again and again throughout the unit; children will hear

Toy Librarians Take Note
If you loan kits to parents, you might want to adapt or even omit some of the written material. This information is oriented to a teacher or family child care provider. I encourage you to add information that would be more supportive to a parent working one-on-one with a child at home.

different things as they become more familiar with the topic. If you are using a binder to organize the paper components of your kit, include the poem in the binder.

Introduction

The introduction for each kit is directed to the teacher. It is a brief summary of the importance of the topic and what you and the children can expect to learn. If you create this kit and will be the only person using it, you probably won't need to include this written piece. If a kit is to be loaned, however, the introduction can ensure quality by helping the teacher who uses it understand your goals in building and using the kit.

Kit contents

I did not break *my* piggy bank to purchase materials for my theme kits. I purchased high-quality materials to build kits for a resource room serving early childhood educators. I know that by the time you purchase half the books I've recommended you will have spent your budget allowance for the year! Please remember that this is a long process. You collect over time. You find books at library sales and yard sales. You receive donated items such as ice-cream makers, dress-up attire, and twinkle lights. Please don't be disheartened by the long list of suggested contents; be inspired to capitalize on what you already own and on what you collect and create.

I've found that my local public library can help me save both time and money. When my research generates lists of books, I request them through the county library system, and the librarians get them for me within a few days. I can look them over and choose only the ones that are most appropriate for the kit I'm working on.

Fact sheet

This section includes basic facts about the theme and, in some cases, tips for the teacher about using the theme; the facts are not intended to be memorized by the children. The purpose of the section is to give teachers some basic information about the topic. We need our brains stimulated too; we know what happens when those brain connections get weak! (If you are loaning kits out and decide to include a sheet like this, it's important that you also make this clear to the user.) The fact sheets might come in handy if children generate some questions. The best thing you can ever say to a child in response to a question is, "I don't know the answer. Let's look it up." You are modeling research skills and showing that it is okay to not have all the information.

Theme tree

Theme trees are discussed in chapter 1. I've included a sample tree with each kit, but you should start with a blank tree and use the ideas in the book only to supplement your own. A blank tree for photocopying is included in appendix 1.

Family involvement

Use this letter to involve the families. Even if it seems that half the parents don't read the stuff we send home, it's important to include those who are willing. This is where the children are your best allies. If they help write the letters, they will make sure their families read them! The letters in this book are samples, not reproducible forms. You will need to tailor each letter to reflect your own plans for the unit.

Ready, set, go!

This section will help you picture your classroom or home environment while you explore a theme. This is where an inventory list of items will become invaluable. Once the materials from the kit are spread throughout your space, you will need this list when it's collection time!

Please note that not all the areas of the room or the routines of the day will reflect the theme. Some areas or routines in each kit are purposely left out. You should only add materials that will enhance meaningful play. If you get carried away with extension ideas, you run the risk of causing children to reject the theme. When your theme is Goldilocks and the Three Bears and you start seeing bears in your sleep, you'll know you've overdone it!

Activity ideas

This is not meant to be an activity book—you have countless other books for that. The handful of ideas suggested for each theme will get you started in a few different areas of the curriculum.

Theme Sources

Fairy tales and folktales

These stories, often set in the distant past, tell of imagined events. They usually include some magical occurrence or character. We have all been introduced to a fascinating cast of giants, trolls, fairies, and witches through these classic tales.

Plan how you will handle the gender bias, violence, and fearful images that are part of most traditional fairy tales. You might be interested in psychologist Bruno Bettelheim's *The Uses of Enchantment: The Meaning and Importance of Fairy Tales* (1976). To remain true to the classic fairy tales, I've included in my lists some versions which have unpleasant images. Please preview all books before reading them to the children, checking for culture, gender, and other forms of bias.

One of my colleagues who teaches three- and four-year-olds gave me a helpful insight. In her experience, many children come to school without an exposure to simple nursery rhymes and folktales. In this case, many of the story versions would be hard to follow without some prior knowledge. For many young children, it might be best to first *tell* the story in its simplest form, perhaps the one you remember from your own childhood. Flannelboard or stick-puppet props would be fine. Let the children create detailed images in their own minds and understand the basic plot before you expose them to varied interpretations and adaptations. The folktales included in this book are "Little Red Riding Hood," "Goldilocks and the Three Bears," and "The Three Billy Boats Gruff."

Traditional themes

You have probably accumulated many resources that would support traditional themes. If so, you might want to concentrate your efforts here for your first few theme kits. A kit is an organizing tool. You already have the great ideas, resources, and play materials—here's your chance to put it all together. The goal with traditional themes is to go beyond the introductory lessons. You'll be amazed at how much information children possess on some of these topics. Take them deeper. Every theme-kit experience should be like taking a trip on the infamous Magic School Bus. You always start at the same place, but you never know where you'll end up.

Favorite story themes

These theme kits tend to be small. They present children with the props to play out a favorite story. By acting as different characters, and using objects that are named in the story, children begin to comprehend the book in a meaningful way. It's one thing to memorize the refrain from *Caps for Sale,* "You monkeys you, you give me back my caps." It's another matter for children to experience many caps flying down from above.

These smaller, story-based kits work well as take-home kits. You might choose to concentrate your efforts on developing a library of take-home kits first. This approach works well if you have limited space.

I strongly encourage children's librarians and toy librarians to build these kits. Maybe if the day comes that Saturday morning commercials feature picture books, we won't have to think about how to engage children in reading. But for now, competition for children's attention is fierce. If books come with appropriate play props, we have a ready audience.

Explorations

This category is inclusive; it leaves no subject behind. If you find yourself intrigued by some man-made or natural object, build a theme kit around it. Whether it's buttons, rocks, dolls, marbles, or wood, it can open windows of learning. These themes might not last as long as some, nor have as many related props. But you might see new passions awakened because of these kits.

Universal themes

What are the shared experiences of the people on this planet? We eat, we sleep, we celebrate, we play; we find shelter, we hunt or gather food, and we clothe ourselves. According to Susan and Jim Stephenson, editors of *The Joyful Child: Essential Montessori for Birth to Three* (2001), it is in the early years, when children are most impressionable, that we should introduce cultures of the world: "[This] is the time to casually introduce these experiences, not with lessons or lectures, but experientially, and sensorially. Through such simple and casual introductions, children come to understand that all humans have the same needs and experiences."

How to Evaluate Your Kits

After each kit is used, it's important to take some time to evaluate your experience with it. Each time you use it with a group of children, you will have a different experience. Try the questions on the "Theme Kit Evaluation" form as a guide to reflecting on each usage, and learn from your experience. The kits will keep getting better as you add and toss contents and improve your approach.

Evaluating Kits That Are Loaned Out

Each time you loan a kit, include an evaluation sheet. The "Theme Kit Evaluation for Borrowers" form includes some suggested questions; please add your own.

Theme Kit Evaluation

Name of Theme Kit _____

What play materials, props, books, and so on, interested children the most?

What should be added to enhance the kit?

Some children wanted to know more about the following:
(If no interests were expressed, how could this be encouraged?)

The families from my group showed interest in the following:

What examples of problem solving did you observe?

Were there enough opportunities for children working with peers and interacting with adults?

What new learning, or reinforcement of past learning, occurred in these general categories?

What basic skills were learned and applied?

Language

Math

Physical (small and large motor)

Social-emotional

Creative

Did you learn anything new about individual children in your class as they responded to the materials and activities?

Materials that did not hold up to heavy use:

Materials that were popular and caused problems with sharing:
(Could they be duplicated?)

What will you do the same way the next time you use this kit?

What would you like to do differently?

Theme Kit Evaluation for Borrowers

Attention Kit User: Please take a few moments to complete this questionnaire and return it with the kit. We will consider your comments and suggestions very seriously and make adaptations as possible. Thanks for sharing.

Name of Theme Kit _____

Are you filling out this evaluation as a parent, teacher, classroom consultant, or other? Please specify your role in the classroom or home. _____

My child/children most enjoyed the following materials and activities:

My child/children wanted to know more about the following:

I wish there were duplicates of the following materials:

Some of the materials were not age-appropriate for my child/children. (Please explain.)

Were there any materials that required too much supervision? Any materials that were hard to keep track of (either because of too many pieces or similarity to what was already available)?

A special project developed out of this theme that might be of interest to other users. (Please describe.)

What additions would you like to see made to this kit?

Any other suggestions?

Why Only Nine Themes?

After you read the ideas for the themes in this book, you'll think to yourself, "Am I rereading a chapter? Something sounds vaguely familiar in this section." Themes are like baking—once you know how to bake a cake, you can bake any cake just by using different ingredients. You are now the expert on theme kits. You have the tools to make any kit that you, the children, and the families want. But before I talk myself out of writing volume two, I'm reminded that people continue to buy cookbooks for new recipes. So I hope we have the chance to meet again over some new theme ideas in the near future!

Snip snap snout, this tale's told out.

Resources

Bettelheim, Bruno. 1976. *The uses of enchantment: The meaning and importance of fairy tales.* New York: Alfred A. Knopf.

Stephenson, Susan, and Jim Stephenson, eds. 2001. *Joyful child: Essential Montessori for birth to three.* Arcata, Calif.: Michael Olaf Montessori Company.

Goldilocks and the Three Bears

Would you like to meet Goldilocks, the girl with golden hair
Who wanders through the woods without a worry or care?

She's very inquisitive, just like you and me,
And wants to know who lives in the house built for three.

Watch what happens when she goes inside
And makes a mess of what she tried.

See the bears' faces change from angry to shocked
As soon as they find sleeping Goldilocks!

If you woke up to three bears staring at you,
What in the world do you think you'd do?

Should Goldilocks tell them she wants to be friends?
Do you think they might invite her back again?

Theme Tree

Physical features
paws
sharp teeth
fur
tail

Bears
American black bear
Asiatic black bear
Malayan sun bear
sloth bear
spectacled bear

Habitats
Set up bear beds using
branches and pine
needles.

Breakfast foods
breakfast graph
Cook oatmeal,
pancakes, eggs.

Size words
big and small
tall and short
thin and thick
long and short
shallow and deep
empty and full

Types of locks
Talk about how Goldilocks got into
the bear's house.
latch
keys and locks
bolts

Setting the table
Learn how to set the table.
What are plates made of? How do
you handle breakable things?
sorting silverware
Create a special placemat for each
bear.

Beds
types of beds
cribs
Japanese futons (different
than American futons)
bunk beds
canopy bed
sleeping bags
cots
mats

Safety lessons
walking alone
going into someone's house uninvited
going into a stranger's house alone,
even if invited

What is Little Bear's chair made of?
Collect other items made from
wood.
What type of worker uses wood?
carpenter
furniture maker
craft artist

Babies
Baby siblings at home? What do they have
that is sized just for them? What did
baby bear have sized just for him?

Questions for discussion
Did you ever break anything? What
happened?
Why did Goldilocks jump out the
window? What would happen if you
jumped from a high place? What do
you do when you are scared?

Introduction

What is it about Goldilocks that endears her to our collective hearts? Is it her lively spirit, her ceaseless curiosity, or her sense of adventure? How many times did we adults want to taste that sweet-smelling bun on the baker's shelf, or flop on the fluffiest-looking bed in the furniture section of the department store, or sit in the driver's seat of a big truck? We didn't dare because we knew about consequences. Here, Goldilocks just goes for it; it's fun to live through her daring adventures without having to suffer the consequences.

Robert Southey first published "The Three Bears" in 1837 in a collection of essays. As much as the simple plot has stayed true to its origins over the years, the intruder's identity has changed multiple times. The uninvited guests have run the gamut from an old woman to a fox to a young girl named Silver-Hair to the familiar Goldilocks (Carpenter 1984, 524). The other part of the story that has been subject to change is the ending. In all the versions I've reviewed, I found few with endings that pleased me.

This is where your children come in. Encourage them to use a fictitious name based on one of their own physical characteristics. Goldilocks was named for her golden hair. Let the children become the character who visits the home of the bears. What would they do inside a bear's home? What would it be like if they visited a family of bears in a cave? How would *they* like the story to end?

This story presents an opportunity to learn facts about bears. After children are introduced to bears and their habitats, they can make up stories to reflect what they've learned. What would polar bears be eating? You might be surprised to learn that their main food is seal. Maybe Goldilocks would visit while they were taking a swim. How would this story end?

The fun of this story lies in its simple props, easy story line, and repetitious language. Unlatch the door and unleash your imagination.

Kit Contents

If children are being introduced to this story for the first time, it is advisable to tell the story in its most basic form before the books are read. Use whatever props you are comfortable with, or none at all. Flannelboard pieces can be made from pictures that are available online. (See "The English Teacher's Assistant" in appendix 2.)

A selection of "The Three Bears" stories

***Goldilocks and the Three Bears* (Hillman)**—This big book, published by Rigby, is a good introduction to this story. The language is simple and traditional. This can also serve as a prereader with its matching small books.

***Goldilocks and the Three Bears: A Tale Moderne* (Guarnaccia)**—The scene for this tale is the bear's split-level home, the food of choice is chili, and the furniture to be explored is based on real pieces from international design artists. The basic story line holds to tradition; the illustrations are a refreshing delight.

***Rolling Along with Goldilocks and the Three Bears* (Meyers)**—This is a creative adaptation of the classic tale in which baby bear uses a wheelchair and a ramp, has a specialized bed, and goes to physical therapy while the porridge is cooling.

***Goldilocks and the Three Bears* (Brett)**—a feast for the eyes. Enjoy the descriptive language and dramatic pictures in this version of the story. The angry expression on the baby bear's face is worth the effort of finding the book.

***Goldilocks and the Three Bears* (Mata)**—This bilingual version is a simple retelling in Spanish.

***Goldilocks and the Three Bears* (Bornstein)**—This version includes sign language illustrations.

***Dusty Locks and the Three Bears* (Lowell)**—This will give you a tickle and a quick introduction to southwestern-style living.

***Leola and the Honeybears* (Rosales)**—This story takes place in the rural South with African American characters.

***Bears Should Share* (Granowsky)**—This flip-me-over book tells the story from Goldilocks' viewpoint and from the little bear's viewpoint.

***Goldilocks and the Three Bears* (Marshall)**—James Marshall offers another offbeat retelling of a favorite tale.

***Abuelo and the Three Bears* (Tello)**—This little paperback is a gem. One half is in Spanish; the other half is in English with the same Latino characters and references. It's a story within a story, with Abuelo (grandfather) entertaining Emilio with the tale of Trencitas (little braids) and her friend Osito (little bear of The Three Bears fame).

***Deep in the Forest* (Turkle)**—A wordless version of "The Three Bears" has one important twist: The bears come into Goldilocks' home uninvited. The dramatically illustrated pictures make it worth a trip to the library.

Stories about bears

***The Grizzly Bear* (Potts)**—This book has very useful information for the teacher to share with interested children. A diagram with labeled body parts is included, along with further resource recommendations.

***Alaska's Three Bears* (Gill)**—This book illustrates the lifestyles of three different species of bears. The borders are rich in thematic detail including additional text of fascinating facts about each type of bear. The story follows three bears through their natural habitats in the Alaskan wilderness.

Sleepy Bears—Mem Fox puts a bed full of bears to sleep with one-of-a-kind rhymes.

***Brown Bear, Brown Bear What Do You See?* (Martin)**

***Bears* from the Animals, Animals series**—This book is a picture and fact-filled reference.

Play props

3 stacking bowls with 3 spoons (teaspoon, tablespoon, serving spoon)

3 chairs or step stools (toddler and adult sizes)

3 beds (child- and adult-size sleeping bags or blankets)

tablecloth or placemats

Commercial products

See appendix 2 for information on how to find products.

The Story Teller "Stage Play" set of eleven masks to act out three fairy tales

Animal Town Finger Fairy Tales finger puppet set, includes Goldilocks and three stylishly attired bears

The Puzzle People's Goldilocks and the Three Bears wood and Velcro storytelling pieces

Learning Curve Interactive Storybooks, Goldilocks and the Three Bears; felt characters and props packed in plastic carry bag

Signs to post

Home Sweet Home

Big Chair/Medium Chair/Baby Chair

Big Bed/Medium Bed/Baby Bed

Bears' House (with an arrow)

The Woods (with an arrow)

Other materials

child-size wheelchair (for use with *Rolling Along with Goldilocks and the Three Bears*); we had one donated by United Cerebral Palsy

futons (Japanese sleeping mats)

Facts about Bears

- Bears are large animals covered with heavy fur. Some of their striking physical features are strong legs, big heads, little eyes, and relatively small ears.
- Bears are smart and curious; they can see and hear like humans and have an acute sense of hearing.
- The eight different kinds of bears in the world are brown bears, American black bears, polar bears, giant panda bears, Asiatic black bears, sloth bears, spectacled bears, and sun bears.
- Sun bears are the smallest bears, and polar bears are the largest bears.
- The colors of bear fur include white (actually translucent), brown, and black.
- Many bears eat nuts, fruits, honey, and fish. A polar bear's diet is largely made up of seals; panda bears eat the leaves of the bamboo plant.
- Mother bears have up to three cubs at a time. Cubs are the size of a small squirrel at birth, and they feed on their mother's milk. The mother bear cares for them for the first few years by teaching them how to hunt for food and be safe from predators.
- During the coldest months, bears go into a deep sleep called *hibernation*. They find or make a place called a *den* to protect them during this time.
- Packs of wolves, large tigers, and walruses are known to kill bears. The greatest enemies of bears are humans. Some people hunt bears for sport.
- The number of bears is dwindling, due in part to the disappearance of bears' natural habitats and to the illegal hunting of bears.
- People in some cultures use bear by-products for making medicine.

Beds for bears

What would it be like for Goldilocks to sleep in a real bear's bed? Here are the "bear" facts about their beds:

- The polar bear digs dens in the icy snow in high places to be able to watch for danger.
- The American black bear makes a bed in a tree or in grassy areas on the ground.
- The brown bear sleeps on the ground because it is too large for most trees.
- The Asiatic bear sleeps in trees in a sitting position.
- The sloth bear makes a bed in a cave during the rainy season, and sleeps in a tree otherwise.

Source: The Bear Den. American Zoo and Aquarium Association, Bear Advisory Group, bearden.org (click on Who's Been Sleeping in My Bed?).

Family Involvement

One way to include families in your program is to write letters. I think it is respectful to children if we include them in the process. At the very least, be sure children know exactly what the letter that is being sent home says, and choose a greeting that includes all the people living in a child's home (mom, dad, grandma, big sister, and so on). Other children might choose to fill in Dear _____ and sign their own names.

Dear _____,

We are learning about the story of Goldilocks and the Three Bears in my class. When you come into my room (child care), would you add your ideas to the Goldilocks Theme Tree? Here are some lessons we will learn:

- facts about bears
- safety tips
- how to make friends
- how to cook porridge

Get ready to ask me these questions:

- The bears' chairs are made from wood. What is made from wood in our home?
- Where did the wood come from?
- Papa Bear used a gruff voice. What does a gruff voice sound like?

Thanks for all your help.

Your daughter (son),

Ready, Set, Go!

Daily routines

Arrival

Post a sign on the front door to your home or classroom: THE HOME OF THE THREE BEARS.

Breakfast

Invite families to bring their porridge recipes.

Circle

Tell the story of The Three Bears. Play the classic game, "We're Going on a Bear Hunt," where children follow your lead repeating words and motions that mimic the adventure of a bear hunt.

Free play

See the interest areas described below.

Small group time

Seriate various items from small to big.

Rest time

Give each child a turn to describe their mat or cot. Is it too hard, too soft, or just right?

Interest areas

Blocks and building

- Provide a variety of toy bears, usually made from soft or hard plastic (available through toy stores, museum shops, educational catalogs, and stores).
- Play with Tree Blocks toy (see appendix 2).

Dramatic play

- Wear bear masks.
- Play with stacking bowls.
- Play with chairs.
- Sleep in beds (sleeping bags).

Manipulative and math center

- Lace beads, smallest to largest.
- Stack cups.
- Stack rings.

Sensory station

- Cook oatmeal.
- Use a megaphone to mimic Papa Bear's loud voice.
- Fill water table or tub with water and large chunks of ice to simulate the Arctic Sea ice, the habitat for polar bears.

Library

- Provide puppets; the Folkmanis company (see appendix 2) has a baby black bear, brown bear, grizzly cub, and polar bear with realistic features.
- Cozy up with a stuffed bear; welcome bears from home.

New discoveries

- Learn about paw prints; ask someone to bring in a child-friendly dog and let children feel pads on paws.

Writing center

- Set up a word bank for sending an apology note to the bears.
- Preaddress envelopes to the Bears' House, in the Woods.
- Dictate an invitation to Goldilocks to come and join the bears for breakfast.

Music and movement

- Sing "Teddy Bear Picnic."
- Discuss how bears move; do they stand upright? Do they move on all four limbs? Mimic their movements with children.

Visitors

- Invite a safety officer to talk to the children about safety rules in their neighborhood.
- Make a booklet of safety tips that each child takes home.

Activity Ideas

Breakfast graph

The bears in the traditional Goldilocks story eat porridge for breakfast. Porridge is a soft food made by boiling oatmeal in water or milk. What do the children and families in your care eat for breakfast? Post a graph on large easel paper, with each child's name written on the long edge and the names or pictures of breakfast foods along the top. The categories for breakfast foods should include cold cereal, oatmeal or hot cereal, eggs, bread or toast, foods that are common to the children in your program, and a category called "other."

Post a new graph each day for the duration of the theme; the results can be tallied each day at circle time. Ideally, a parent can help the child fill in the graph as they arrive each morning. Leave a space under each child's name for family members to record their own breakfasts.

If children are served breakfast at school, create a similar graph or table illustrating the frequency with which various food items are served for the duration of the theme.

"This porridge is too hot!"

Find out why Goldilocks liked the temperature of baby bear's porridge best. Fill three bowls of different sizes with oatmeal. The largest bowl will have the most oatmeal; the baby bear's bowl will have a very small serving. Which one cools off the fastest? You can tell best by looking for steam or feeling with your finger. Don't let children burn their tongues!

Have a "hot and cold" sorting activity. Prepare two empty boxes, one labeled "hot" and one labeled "cold." Ask parents to help you collect magazine pictures of items that symbolize hot and cold. Glue only the top edge of each picture to a square piece of oaktag, and write the correct term ("hot" or "cold") on the oaktag underneath the picture. On the back of the oaktag you can write the name of the item. These cards might include a toaster, a stove, a refrigerator, ice, a Popsicle, an icicle, a polar bear, and a sun. Always include items that are familiar to the children and the cultures they represent.

Ask the children to sort the cards. They can check each answer by carefully lifting the picture (from the side that is not glued down) and looking for the word "hot" or "cold" underneath.

Blubber mitten

Do this experiment to demonstrate the insulation quality of blubber.

Materials

shortening
2 reclosable sandwich bags
a bowl of cold water with ice cubes

Directions

Fill one of the bags about one-third full of shortening, then turn the other bag inside out. Place it inside the bag with the shortening so that the zippers match and you are able to zip one bag to the other. Now you have a "blubber mitten" to put your hand in.

Have each child feel how cold the water is with their bare hands. Let each child take a turn placing one hand in the mitten and then putting it in the ice water. How does the water feel with the blubber mitten on?

Talk about other animals that also have a layer of blubber: walrus, whale, and seal. Do you live in a climate where a layer of blubber would be helpful?

Source: www.teelfamily.com (click on Activities, Polar Bear and the Walrus)

Find a bear chair

This game is similar to musical chairs without the competition.

- Set up two rows of chairs back to back with enough room to walk around the perimeter.
- Play the song "Teddy Bear Picnic" or other lively music.
- Encourage children to prance or lumber around the chairs until you stop the music.
- Everyone sits in a chair as soon as the music stops.
- Start at any chair and have children take turns saying, in a repeating pattern, "papa bear's chair," "mama bear's chair," or "baby bear's chair," until everyone has had a chance to speak. If you're in the pretend papa bear chair, use a great big voice; in mama bear's chair, use a medium voice; and in baby bear's chair, use a wee little voice.
- Start the music and the prancing again. Children will enjoy using their different voices each time they sit in a new seat.

Bear place settings

How would you set a table for a family of bears? Start with bear placemats, of course.

Materials

large piece of oaktag for each child, or use file folders opened flat

scraps cut from colored or patterned self-adhesive paper

paper plates or bowls in a variety of sizes

paper cups in a variety of sizes

glue

pictures of food

drawing implements

Directions

Decorate the oaktag with precut scraps of self-adhesive paper. Children can choose a plate or bowl and a cup of matching size to glue onto their mat. Let them cut out pictures or draw the foods representing a bear's diet on the plate. Based on the size of the plate and cup, they can identify whether it's for papa, mama, or baby bear.

Resources

Barton, Byron. 1991. *The three bears.* New York: Harper Collins.

Bornstein, Harry, and Karen L. Saulnier. 1990. *Goldilocks and the three bears: Told in signed English.* Washington, D.C.: Gallaudet University Press, Kendall Green Publications.

Brett, Jan. 1987. *Goldilocks and the three bears.* New York: Dodd, Mead & Company.

Carpenter, Humphrey, and Mari Prichard. 1984. *The Oxford companion to children's literature.* Oxford: Oxford University Press.

Cauley, Lorinda Bryan. 1981. *Goldilocks and the three bears.* New York: G. P. Putnam's Sons.

Dabcovich, Lydia. 1997. *The polar bear son: An Inuit tale.* New York: Clarion Books.

Ernst, Lisa Campbell. 2000. *Goldilocks returns.* New York: Simon and Schuster.

Fox, Mem. 1999. *Sleepy bears.* New York: Harcourt Brace.

Gill, Shelley R. 1990. *Alaska's three bears.* Seattle: Sasquatch Books.

Granowsky, Alvin. 1996. *Bears should share.* Austin, Tex.: Steck-Vaughn Company.

Guarnaccia, Steven. 1999. *Goldilocks and the three bears: A tale moderne.* New York: Harry N. Abrams, Inc.

Helmer, Diana Star. 1997. *Black bears.* New York: Powerkids Press.

Hillman, Janet. 1996. *Goldilocks and the three bears.* Crystal Lake, Ill.: Rigby.

Lodge, Bernard. 1998. *Mouldylocks.* Boston: Houghton Mifflin Company.

Lowell, Susan. 2001. *Dusty Locks and the three bears: Portraits of art.* New York: Henry Holt and Co.

Marshall, James. 1998. *Goldilocks and the three bears.* New York: Penguin Books.

Martin Jr., Bill. 1983. *Brown bear, brown bear, what do you see?* New York: Holt, Rinehart and Winston.

Mata, Marta. 1998. *Goldilocks and the three bears/Ricitos de Oro y los tres osos.* San Francisco: Chronicle Books.

Meyers, Cindy. 1999. *Rolling along with Goldilocks and the three bears.* Bethesda, Md.: Woodbine House, Inc.

Potts, Steve. 1997. *Wildlife of North America: The grizzly bear.* Mankato, Minn.: Capstone Press.

Rosales, Melodye Benson. 1999. *Leola and the honeybears.* New York: Scholastic, Inc.

Schwabacher, Martin. 2001. *Bears.* Animals Animals Series. New York: Benchmark Books.

Tello, Jerry. 1997. *Abuelo and the three bears.* New York: Scholastic Inc.

Turkle, Brinton. 1976. *Deep in the forest.* New York: E. P. Dutton.

Little Red Riding Hood

The story of Little Red Riding Hood is often told;
Some characters are scary, some young, some old.

It's the tale of a girl who walks alone in the woods
And doesn't listen to her mother as well as she should.

She wanders from the path and talks to a stranger;
Her mother told her that could mean danger!

A wolf appears and acts friendly and caring;
Should Little Red Riding Hood have been so daring?

She visits her grandmom with a basket of treats
And is fearful when she sees BIG FURRY FEET!

How will the story end? Read it and see
If the problem is solved nonviolently.

Can the woodcutter use conflict resolution
To bring this story to a peaceful conclusion?

You be the judge, read it and see
If everyone goes home, safe and happy.

Theme Tree

The color red
Red is Best (Stinson 1982)
Fill Red Riding Hood's
basket with red foods.

Grandparents
cultural terms—nana, *bubbe,*
zeydah, pop-pop, mom-
mom, *abuela,* nanny

Conflict resolution

Sickness and health
get-well cards—in writing
center
Cook chicken soup.

Wolves
as character in fairy tales and stories
legend of Romulus and Remus—tale
of babies raised by wolves
new language—pack (a pack of
wolves), loping (how wolves
move), den (their home), howl
(their cry), cub (their young)
fable—"The Boy Who Cried Wolf"
types of wolves—gray wolf,
timber wolf

Safety rules
rules for city life (traffic, strangers)—
Would Little Red Riding Hood
meet a wolf in the city? What
might she run into? What animal
would she see in a rainforest?
rules for rural life (animal dangers,
wooded areas)

Family traditions
visiting grandparents, living
with grandparents
foods for special occasions

Questions for discussion
The wolf tricks Little Red Riding
Hood. Has anyone ever tricked
you into believing something
that wasn't true?

Capes
magician's cape
superhero cape
Halloween costume cape
nurse's cape (part of uniform
in history)

Introduction

Reading an assortment of Little Red Riding Hood stories is a little like playing the children's game "Whisper Down the Lane." The more times it is transcribed, the more possibilities emerge. The first known recording of the tale dates from 1697, "Le Petit Chaperon Rouge" (The Little Red Hood), by French writer Charles Perrault. In this story, a little girl takes custard and a pot of butter to her sick grandmother. This story ends abruptly with the little girl being eaten by the wolf. The brothers Grimm version, "Little Red Cap," added a snoring wolf, a hunter, and a sack of stones to fill the wolf's belly. It will be up to you to discover the limitless interpretations of this story. "Folktales (and fairytales), by their very nature are fluid and change as they are passed from generation to generation. The truth about Little Red Riding Hood is the truth about all great stories. They demand that we play with them, personalize them, bring them to life. Each generation must retell them" (Rovenger 1993).

The tale of Little Red Riding Hood is full of lessons about caring, bravery, nature, safety, and adventure. Although the wolf is personified and portrayed as heinous, and the woods as a scary, foreboding place, the book presents an opportunity to seek more accurate images. The English adaptation of a Chinese version, *Lon Po Po,* offers this dedication:

> *To all the wolves of the world*
> *for lending their good name*
> *as a tangible symbol*
> *for our darkness.*
> (Young 1996)

This kit contains materials to portray the wolf in its natural habitat, as a member of the wild dog family. The woods can be viewed as adventurous without the fear tactics. Children can discover their own strengths and family traditions while play-acting the story. You'll notice that Little Red Riding Hood carries different food depending on the story setting. Be forewarned that the French version (Martin 1998) has the granddaughter carrying a bottle of wine to make the grandmother feel better. Be prepared to answer questions that might arise.

Kit Contents

If children are being introduced to this story for the first time, it is advisable to tell the story in its most basic form before the books are read. Use whatever props you are comfortable with or none at all.

A selection of Little Red Riding Hood stories

***Little Red Riding Hood: A Newfangled Prairie Tale* (Ernst)**—This Red Riding Hood rides her bike through the prairie and takes healthy muffins to Grandma, who rides a tractor and takes care of herself. Everyone's a winner at the end of this story.

***Lon Po Po: A Red Riding Hood Story from China* (Young)**—Three brave sisters outsmart the wolf.

***Little Red Riding Hood* (Moroney)**—Lamaze Infant Development System board book; richly colored drawings are the perfect complement to this simple tale told in verse.

***Little Red Riding Hood* (Martin)**—A little French girl visits her grand-mother with pie and wine; the wolf is cut open to release the girl and her grandmother.

***Picture Me As Little Red Riding Hood* (Dandi)**—This board book has space for a child's photo, so that the child plays the part of Red Riding Hood. The child shames the wolf into an apology and celebrates with apple pie for all!

***Little Red Riding Hood* story and cassette (Fox)**—The main character is Yvonne, an African American girl who wears a hooded cape of the finest velvet and goes off to visit Grandma in this contemporary version. Her clever friends save the day.

***Little Red Riding Hood: Told in Signed English* (Bornstein)**—In this version the grandmother hides in the closet and the hunter shoots the wolf to keep him away from Red Riding Hood.

***Little Red Riding Hood, Jumbled Tumbled Tales and Rhymes* (Giles)**—This is available as a big book with matching, small beginning readers. Red Riding Hood is rescued by a female woodcutter. There is no violence.

***Red Riding Hood's Math Adventure* (Harcourt and Wortzman)**—This is an interactive book that teaches simple subtraction as Red Riding Hood gives cookies from her basket to all the surprise characters she meets on her journey.

***Caperucita Roja* (Hutchinson)**—The story is told in Spanish with very simple language. The main words and phrases are illustrated in the *vocabulario* section. The story ends nonviolently.

Little Red Riding Hood **video by Happily Ever After Fairy Tales for Every Child**—This video from the Happily Every After Fairy Tales for Every Child series uses the voices from a diverse group of famous stars telling everyday fairy tales that have an ethnic twist. This version features an Asian girl, Little Red Happy Coat, who visits her grandmom, Poa-Poa, and fights off the wolf with help from the village herbalist. Unfortunately, the illustrations of Red Happy Coat are stereotypical.

A Book of Fruit **(Lember)**—This book teaches the origins of food, and does it beautifully. Use it to support the development of "food" as a subtopic in the Red Riding Hood theme.

Stories about grandparents

The Patchwork Quilt **(Flourney)**—Tanya finds a special way to help her sick grandmother.

Abuela **(Dorros)**—Available in Spanish or English, this is a fantasy story about a Hispanic girl and her grandmother having an adventure in New York City.

Stories about wolves

It is important to include books that represent wolves in their natural habitat without wily and evil personification.

Wolves **(Gibbons)**—Detailed and realistic drawings support the simply stated facts about wolves' natural habitat.

Big Wolf and Little Wolf **(Denslow)**—A family of wolves are the stars of this endearing fictional story. Perfect for toddlers and preschoolers.

Look to the North: A Wolf Pup Diary **(George)**—Beautiful illustrations and diary entries describe a day in the life of a litter of wolf pups.

The Big Backyard **and** *Ranger Rick*—These respected children's magazines can be searched for wolves photographed in their natural surroundings and for factual information.

Stories that feature life in the woods

This is an opportunity for children to learn about animals that live in the woods, wildflowers, and other treasures.

In the Woods: Who's Been Here? **(George)**—Breathtaking illustrations of a realistic walk through the woods fill this book.

"Stopping by Woods on a Snowy Evening" (poem by Robert Frost)— "The woods are lovely, dark, and deep . . . ." Enjoy this journey through the woods, very different from Red Riding Hood's walk except for one thing: They both had promises to keep.

Forest sounds on cassette tape or compact disc—Many tapes exist for purchase or loan at your library. *The Four Seasons,* a classical composition by Vivaldi, would also be suitable.

Play props

capes of different colors and fabrics

eyeglasses for the grandmother

nightgown

farmer's attire (for the prairie grandmother—see *Little Red Riding Hood: A Newfangled Prairie Tale)*

baskets—try wicker for authenticity

flowers—silk or plastic for collecting in the woods (available at craft stores)

foods to be brought to the grandmother

bed—use a cot with a blanket as the grandmother's bed

Commercial products

See appendix 2 for information on how to find products.

Folkmanis puppets—a perfect story wolf and a more realistic timber wolf puppet

Woodkins Little Red Riding Hood interactive wooden activity set

The Story Teller "Stage Play" set of eleven masks to act out three fairy tales

Totline and Felt Wonders (found in educational toy stores and catalogs)—flannel pieces to tell the story

Finger Puppet Story Set (Little Red Riding Hood and other tales told with gentler endings) from Constructive Playthings

Signs to post

WOODS

BEWARE OF WOLVES

GRANDMOTHER'S HOUSE—2 MILES

CLOSET (to hide in)

Other materials

baskets and containers, a variety for transporting foods representing various cultures

photos of women and children from African villages carrying baskets filled with produce on their heads; see *Handa's Surprise,* by Eileen Browne, in which Handa carries a basket of fruit on her head

photos of wolves in natural surroundings

quilts and blankets to cover Grandmother; materials and designs used for quilts will vary depending on place of origin

Facts about Wolves

- Wolves make their homes on prairies, in forests, and on mountains.

- For dens, they use caves, hollow tree trunks, or holes they dig in the ground. A den is also called a lair.

- Full-grown wolves weigh up to 175 pounds.

- The length of an adult wolf varies from 5.5 feet to 6.5 feet, measuring from nose to tip of tail.

- Wolves belong to the dog family. Their prominent features are powerful teeth, bushy tails, and round pupils.

- Wolves are carnivores; their diet includes berries, small animals, birds, and animals as large as sheep and reindeer.

- Wolves are social animals; they move together in packs.

- Wolves express their emotions through movements of their facial muscles, eyes, ears, and nose.

- Wolves protect their territory by urinating around its perimeter.

- Female wolves have up to eleven pups in each litter. Parent wolves regurgitate food that has been partially digested to feed their young.

Source: Microsoft Encarta 98, Microsoft Corporation.

Family Involvement

One way to include families in your program is to write letters. I think it is respectful to children if we include them in the process. At the very least, be sure children know exactly what the letter that is being sent home says, and choose a greeting that includes all the people living in a child's home (mom, dad, grandma, big sister, and so on). Other children might choose to fill in Dear _____ and sign their own names.

Dear _____,

We are learning about the story of Little Red Riding Hood in my class (child care). When you come into my room, would you add your ideas to the Red Riding Hood Theme Tree?

Do you have any of the following materials to loan or give to our class to help us enjoy this theme?

- wicker baskets
- artificial flowers
- real flowers for us to keep in water and observe
- cape
- fruits or vegetables that we like to eat at our house
- small quilt or blanket used to cover Red Riding Hood's grandmother

Here are some of the activities and lessons we will be doing:

- learning about real wolves and their habitats
- dramatizing the story
- practicing solving problems without violence
- talking about how to take care of our own grandparents

Get ready to ask me these questions at the end of this unit of study:

- What foods do you think our grandmother would like to eat?
- How do wolves take care of their pups?
- Where do wolves live?
- What should you do if a stranger approaches you?

Thanks for all your help.

Your daughter (son),

Ready, Set, Go!

Daily routines

Arrival

Invite children to bring small baskets filled with one type of fruit or vegetable. Be sure the "surprise" food is covered by a napkin.

Circle

Children take turns giving a clue about what food is in their basket. Who can guess?

Free play

See the interest areas described below.

Outdoor play

Children take baskets outside to collect things. Little Red Riding Hood picked flowers on her walk. What would the children like to pretend to collect? If they collect for real, review safety and environmental concerns.

Small group time

Bake muffins to take to a senior care center or nursing home in the area.

Rest time

Listen to a recording of nature sounds from a forest setting. Many commercial tapes are available. Do a search online or visit your library for ideas.

Interest areas

Blocks and building

- Add small woodland animals (Constructive Playthings animal set includes raccoon, beaver, skunk, and more).
- Add tree stumps and small branches.

Dramatic play

- Refer to the dress-up items and accessories listed in Kit Contents. In addition to the predictable red cape, provide props to broaden the story. Change the name of the story to Little Blue Riding Hood; try to encourage children to see this character as a boy. Why not? At Halloween you can find a variety of capes to add to your kit.

Manipulative and math center

- Sort and count flowers.

Art and projects

- Provide a mural-size paper for children to paint trees, which can become a forest scene in the blocks or dramatic play area.
- Have children cut out flower pictures from garden catalogs.
- Create a patchwork quilt for Grandmom. Each child decorates a square of felt, fabric, or paper.

Sensory station

- Provide rocks and a scale. (Rocks were used to fill the wolf's belly in some versions of this tale.)

Library

- See the list of books in Kit Contents.
- Add a Storytime finger puppet set.
- Add Folkmanis puppets.

New discoveries

- Discover the softness of moss, which grows naturally in shaded, moist areas. Dried Spanish moss is available at garden stores.

Writing center

- Provide materials and word bank to make get-well cards for Grandmother.

Music and movement

- Scatter paper or artificial flowers outside; each child has a basket (from home) or bag (with handle cut out to look like a basket); children meander through the woods, picking up flowers.

Activity Ideas

Field trip

Plan a trip to a park or a nature center. Learn about safety in the woods. Little Red Riding Hood picked wildflowers in the woods. Take a walk wearing a masking tape bracelet. Wrap 2-inch-wide masking tape, sticky-side out, around each child's wrist. Their dominant hand should be free to pick nature's gifts and use them to decorate their bracelets. It is important that you review with the children what can and cannot be collected from outside.

Meet a woodcutter

Why do woodcutters chop wood? In some Red Riding Hood stories, a woodcutter saves the day. Do children know why a woodcutter would be in a forest? In the story, what tool does the woodcutter use? Help the children learn how trees are used, from tree trunk to cut wood to wood products. Set up a discovery area of objects made from wood. Include pencils, rainstick, wooden toys, puzzles, rulers, and birdhouses. Invite a carpenter or woodcraft artist to your class.

Children can make musical instruments out of wood. Collect small blocks of wood from a local home improvement center or lumberyard to make sand blocks. Demonstrate how to sand a piece of wood to smooth the rough spots. Help children use a small hammer and carpet tacks to adhere rough sandpaper to one surface of each piece of wood. To play, rub two blocks together to make a shuffling sound.

Story quilt

It's easier than you think to make a story quilt using photographs or children's pictures. Choose a specific topic for your quilt. Some ideas include facts about wolves, your children's version of this fairy tale, or stories about grandparents. Copy pictures or photographs onto transfer paper (copying stores carry this paper) and then press onto fabric with an iron or heat press. Sew fabric squares together.

Resources

Bornstein, Harry, and Karen L. Saulnier. 1990. *Little Red Riding Hood: Told in signed English.* Washington, D.C.: Gallaudet University Press, Kendall Green Publications.

Browne, Eileen. 1999. *Handa's surprise.* Cambridge, Mass.: Candlewick Press.

Carpenter, Humphrey, and Mari Prichard. 1984. *The Oxford companion to children's literature.* Oxford: Oxford University Press.

Dandi. 1997. *Picture me as Little Red Riding Hood.* Akron, Ohio: Picture Me Books, Inc.

Denslow, Sharon Phillips. 2000. *Big Wolf and Little Wolf.* New York: Greenwillow.

Dorros, Arthur. 1991. *Abuela.* New York: Dutton.

Ernst, Lisa Campbell. 1995. *Little Red Riding Hood: A newfangled prairie tale.* New York: Simon and Schuster.

Flournoy, Valerie. 1985. *The patchwork quilt.* New York: Dial Books.

Fox, Naomi. 1993. *Little Red Riding Hood.* Studio City, Calif.: Confetti Entertainment Company.

Frost, Robert. 1978. *Stopping by woods on a snowy evening.* Illustrated by Susan Jeffers. New York: E. P. Dutton.

George, Jean Craighead. 1997. *Look to the north: A wolf pup diary.* New York: HarperCollins.

George, Lindsay Barrett. 1995. *In the woods: Who's been here?* New York: Greenwillow Books.

Gibbons, Gail. 1994. *Wolves.* New York: Holiday House.

Giles, Jenny. 1998. *Little Red Riding Hood.* Crystal Lake, Ill.: Children's Television Workshop and Rigby.

Happily Ever After Fairy Tales. 1995. *Little Red Riding Hood.* Video. New York: Random House, Inc.

Harcourt, Lalie, and Ricki Wortzman. 2001. *Red Riding Hood's math adventure.* Watertown, Mass.: Charlesbridge Publishing.

Hutchinson, Hanna. 1995. *Caperucita Roja.* Cincinnati: Another Language Press.

Isadora, Rachel. 1998. *A South African night.* New York: Greenwillow Books.

Lember, Barbara Hirsch. 1994. *A book of fruit.* New York: Ticknor and Fields Books for Young Readers.

Lewin, Betsy. 1993. *Yo, hungry wolf! A nursery rap.* New York: Doubleday Books for Young Readers.

Martin, Jean-Francois. 1998. *Little Red Riding Hood.* New York: Abbeville Press, Inc.

Microsoft Corporation. Microsoft Encarta 98.

Moroney, Tracey. 1999. *Little Red Riding Hood.* Chicago: Learning Curve International, Inc.

Rovenger, Judith. 1993. The better to hear you with: Making sense of folktales. *School Library Journal* (March): 135.

Stinson, Kathy. 1982. *Red is best.* Toronto: Annick Press.

Turkle, Brinton. 1976. *Deep in the forest.* New York: E. P. Dutton.

Young, Ed. 1996. *Lon Po Po: A Red Riding Hood story from China.* New York: Penguin Putnam Books for Young Readers.

Farm

Have you heard of Old McDonald? He has a farm
Where the rooster crows early like a morning alarm.

Farmers wake up early to get their chores done
And finish all their work before the rising sun.

Farmers' children wake up to the morning dew
And don't eat breakfast until the chores are through.

If you lived on a farm, you'd have chores every day:
Collect the eggs, milk the cows, and feed the horses hay.

Shear the sheep, feed the chickens, clean the pig pen,
Fix the tractor, mend the fence, work 'til day's end.

I'm sure you have jobs at home to help your family.
It's important to do your part and help out willingly.

Let's pretend to be farmers who live on a farm
With animals, crops to grow, and a big red barn!

We'll work from dawn to dusk, until the jobs are done,
And bring the food to market to feed everyone.

Theme Tree

Animals
sounds they make
physical characteristics
family names
uses on a farm

Kinds of animals
cows
pigs
sheep—*Charlie Needs a Cloak,* wool, weaving
loom
horses
dog
cat
chickens
geese/ducks

Rural life
versus city life

Equipment on a farm
auger
combine
tractor
drill
elevator

Growing things
vegetables
fruit trees
grains
nuts

Places on a farm
barn
farm house
silo
horse stalls
bins—round concrete or metal structures used to store grain
pond
pig pen
chicken coop
pasture

From farm to table
Learn how all the farm products get to market.
Match animals with their food products and by-products.
dairy products
recipes

Songs and rhymes
Old McDonald Had a Farm
Farmer Brown's Cow (Kididdles Web site for lyrics)
Hey Diddle Diddle
Little Boy Blue
Baa Baa Black Sheep
Mary Had a Little Lamb
I Had a Rooster
There Was a Farmer Had a Dog
Go Tell Aunt Rhody
Five Little Ducks

Chores
chores on a farm
chores at home

Introduction

I don't think a single child in America leaves preschool without learning about farm animals. Farms have joined the technological age. Not much of the work is done by hand anymore. Milking stools might soon become extinct. But no matter how high tech the industry becomes, this is still a fact every child must know: Cows produce milk. Children these days are so far removed from the origins of food that a caregiver can help to make those connections.

In this kit, children will feel wool from a sheep, touch hay, and see what is meant by "down" in a "down comforter." Hopefully, they'll never dump the last of their milk down the drain again, and they will have gained a new appreciation for the art of farming.

Children will learn names of farm machines, be introduced to each animal, and find out that on a real farm nobody would let the Little Red Hen bake bread all by herself.

Set your alarm for 4:00 A.M., put on your overalls, eat a nice big breakfast, and meet us in the barn.

Kit Contents

A selection of farm stories

Big Red Barn **(Brown)**—These animals like to play while the children are away and have been doing so since this book was first published in 1956!

The Little Red Hen **(Galdone)**—You can almost smell the bread baking at the end of this story; the hen takes you from a grain of wheat to the finished loaf while her lazy housemates look on.

Rosie's Walk **(Hutchins)**—Bold illustrations will keep your attention as Rosie the hen unknowingly takes the hungry fox through a series of mishaps on her stroll around the farm.

The Milk Makers **(Gibbons)**—Leave it to Gail Gibbons to offer this level of detail and accuracy for young children.

Charlie Needs a Cloak **(dePaola)**—The sheep is sheared; the wool is carded and spun, woven into cloth, and dyed red to make a cloak.

Pigs **(Miller)**—See the complete series of True Books by Sara Swan Miller, which includes chickens, cows, sheep, and goats.

Midnight Farm **(Simon)**—Singer Carly Simon turns children's book writer and takes her readers on a silly romp through a New England barnyard late one night.

The Usborne Book of Farm Animals **(Everett)**—Suitable for a toddler, this book uses large, realistic illustrations of familiar farm animals.

Play props

denim overalls

flannel shirts

milking stool

milking pail

plastic eggs and a basket for collecting eggs

garden tools (trowel, hoe, spade)

watering can

buckets

work gloves

costume accessories to represent farm animals (animal noses, headbands with ears)

Commercial products

set of soft vinyl farm animals, should have realistic features and be scaled to size

barn and accessories

Folkmanis puppets (see appendix 2)

wooden farm puzzles

Signs to post

Barn

Chicken Coop

PIG PEN

HORSE STALL

WASH YOUR HANDS AFTER TOUCHING THE ANIMALS!

HAY FOR SALE

Other materials

garden stool or one-leg milking stool

old-fashioned berry basket

aluminum milk can

grinders to grind the wheat like The Little Red Hen

samples of four phases of sheep's fleece:

> unprocessed fleece (feel the natural lanolin)
> processed wool
> yarn
> clothing made from wool

cotton plant

down and something down-filled (jacket, quilt)

Facts about Farms

- Biotechnology is increasing crop productivity.
- The most important food-energy source for three-fourths of the world population is grains. Grains are grown for their edible seeds such as wheat, rice, corn, oats, and barley.
- The temperate, subtropical, and tropical regions of the world all grow important fruit crops. Apples, pears, peaches, plums, nectarines, and cherries are the major temperate fruits. Oranges, lemons, limes, tangerines, olives, and figs are subtropical crops. The leading tropical fruits include bananas, avocados, mangoes, dates, pineapples, and papayas.
- Peanuts and coconuts are the most important nut crops and are common sources of food and edible oils.
- More than forty types of vegetables are grown worldwide, including leafy salad crops, root crops (beets, carrots, potatoes), cole crops (cabbage, broccoli), and others that produce a fruit or seed (tomato, peas, corn).
- The vacuum milking machine now does the work the farmer used to do.
- Purebred milk cows raised in the United States are the Holstein, Friesian, Guernsey, Jersey, Ayrshire, and Brown Swiss.
- The amount of butterfat in milk varies among different animals:
    Holstein cow milk 3.5–3.8 percent
    Jersey cow milk 4.0–5.0 percent
    Sheep milk 7.0–7.5 percent
    Goat milk 3.5–4.0 percent
- Wool comes from the soft fleece of sheep. One pound of wool can be spun into twenty miles of yarn.
- A lamb recognizes her mother among all the sheep by the bleating sound.
- Each mature female sheep produces 7–10 pounds of sheared wool a year.
- Meat from a cow is called beef, meat from a sheep is mutton, and meat from a pig is pork.
- A female cow is a heifer until she produces a calf, then she is called a cow.
- A male cow is called a bull or a steer.
- A baby cow is a calf.
- Some species of cows weigh an average of 1,300 pounds when full grown.
- Female sheep are ewes.
- Male sheep are rams or wethers.
- A baby sheep is a lamb.
- Female pigs are gilts until they give birth; then they are called sows.
- Male pigs are boars or barrows.
- A baby pig is called a piglet or pig.
- A pig can weigh as much as 250 pounds at six months of age.

Sources: Microsoft Encarta 98, Microsoft Corporation; www.strausmilk.com; www.10acresbackyard.com.

Family Involvement

One way to include families in your program is to write letters. I think it is respectful to children if we include them in the process. At the very least, be sure children know exactly what the letter that is being sent home says, and choose a greeting that includes all the people living in a child's home (mom, dad, grandma, big sister, and so on). Other children might choose to fill in Dear _____ and sign their own names.

Dear _____,

We are learning all about farms in my class. When you come into my room (child care), would you add your ideas to the Farm Theme Tree?

Do you have any of these materials to loan or give to our class to help us enjoy this theme?

- wool yarn
- weaving loom
- clothes made from wool or cotton
- hand-powered food grinder

Here are some activities we will be doing:

- making butter
- making applesauce
- learning how to weave
- learning how to milk a cow
- experimenting with eggs

Get ready to ask me these questions at the end of the unit of study:

- What animals live on a farm? What kind of food do we get from farm animals?
- Do you think you'd like to work on a farm? Why or why not?
- Why do pigs roll in the mud?

Thanks for all your help.

Your daughter (son),

Ready, Set, Go!

Daily routines

Arrival

Encourage children to make a barnyard sound to announce their arrival. This is completely optional, and some children will not be comfortable doing this. They can introduce themselves as Jennifer Lamb with their mom or dad sheep or Casey Calf with mom or dad cow.

Breakfast

Prepare a breakfast fit for a hardworking farmer.

Circle

Introduce this topic by reading the poem or one of the books from the Kit Contents list. Sing some of your favorite farm songs.

Free choice

See the interest areas described below.

Outdoor play

If possible, add a pile of hay to the play yard. Pretend the climbing equipment is a barn with a loft. Bring out birdseed to feed the birds, just as farmers feed the chickens. Think about what "crops" you could grow.

Small group time

Make butter, bake fruit muffins (talk about the ingredients that come from a farm), or do a simple weaving project.

Lunch

Make a chart listing the lunch foods and where they came from. As time goes on, fewer and fewer children should say, "From the grocery store."

Rest time

Explain to the children that it is a good idea to take a rest in the heat of the day (depending on the season). Many farmers do their work in the early morning and early evening, although many also work all day long.

Interest areas

Blocks and building

- Provide indoor-outdoor carpet that has a grasslike texture.
- Provide a set of farm animals.
- Provide pictures of farms (try to find a calendar that features farms).
- Use oatmeal containers for silos or grain bins.
- Add farm equipment such as toy tractors or trucks to take the food to market.

Dramatic play

- See play props listed in Kit Contents.

Manipulative and math center

- Teach the concept of a *dozen:* a dozen eggs, a dozen cookies.
- Use the song/rhyme "Farmer Brown Has Ten Green Apples" as the basis for a flannelboard activity:

Farmer Brown has 10 green apples hanging from his tree,
Farmer Brown has 10 green apples hanging from his tree,
And he plucked one apple and he ate it hungrily.

Now Farmer Brown has 9 green apples hanging from his tree,
Now Farmer Brown has 9 green apples hanging from his tree,
And he plucked one apple . . .

Art and projects

- Make vegetable and fruit prints.
- Make a scarecrow as a group project.

Sensory station

- Explore and sort seeds and beans: pumpkin, sunflower, dried lima beans, black-eyed peas, and so on.
- Encourage mud-making outside.
- Explore feathers. Do they float? Why?
- Taste milk products.
- Provide products made from farm animal hides (leather, sheepskin).

Library

- See list of books in Kit Contents.
- Add garden catalogs to the bookshelf.
- Use hay bales for extra seating.

New discoveries

- Contact local farms to see if they will provide an egg incubator and technical support. It is important to plan what you will do after the chicks hatch.

Writing center

- Write questions about farms, farm animals, and farm life and send them to a farmer. (Many farms are listed on the Internet.)

Music and movement

Tell each child to choose one animal sound to make. Practice the basic farm animal sounds. Children should pretend they are moving around the barnyard making their chosen sound. As all the children move around making sounds, they seek out their own kind. Once all the animals have found their matches, all the sounds stop.

Activity ideas

Set up a farm stand

Everybody enjoys shopping at a roadside farm stand. Treat your families to a stand selling fresh baked items and produce at the end of the day. Set up a table with baskets of fresh produce, a scale (can be pretend), and a cash box. Children can make signs with prices. Be sure to write on the signs that the products are fresh from the farm!

Corn husking

Husk it, cook it, and eat it!

Apple sorting

Bring a basket filled with a variety of apples. Children can sort, count, and have a tasting party.

Milk the Cow

Give the children the experience of milking a cow by creating these pretend udders.

Use a pencil tip to punch a hole in the bottom of a paper cup (unwaxed works best).

Use a pin to prick holes in the fingertips of a surgical glove. Do not use the thumb (cows have four teats). Tie the thumb off in a knot.

Place the open end of the glove around the bottom of the cup and tape it with duct tape.

Fill the cup half full with water and let it drip down to the "teats."

While the teacher holds the cup, a child uses thumb and forefinger to force the water (milk) down and out.

(Adapted from Straus Family Creamery, www.strausmilk.com)

Eggs-periment

This egg experiment will get your children's attention!

Use a glass milk bottle (available at most supermarkets).

Put a peeled hard-boiled egg on the mouth of the bottle and gently try to push the egg into the bottle without breaking it. It doesn't fit.

Now, place the egg in cold water.

Fill the milk bottle with hot water for a couple minutes and empty it out. If the water temperature is controlled in your classroom, it may be difficult to get the tap water hot enough to make this work. While the bottle is still hot from the water, and the egg is cold, put it back on top of the bottle with the narrow end down.

The egg should get sucked right in. The difference in the temperatures creates suction, which pulls the egg through the narrow opening.

(Adapted from Straus Family Creamery, www.strausmilk.com)

Resources

Brown, Margaret Wise. 1995. *Big red barn*. New York: HarperCollins.

dePaola, Tomie. 1982. *Charlie needs a cloak*. New York: Simon and Schuster.

Dunn, Judy, and Phoebe Dunn. 1981. *The animals of Buttercup Farm*. New York: Random House.

Everett, Felicity. 1993. *The Usborne book of farm animals*. Tulsa: Educational Development Corporation Publishing.

Galdone, Paul. 1972. *The little red hen*. New York: Houghton Mifflin Co.

Gibbons, Gail. 1986. *The milk makers*. New York: Simon and Schuster Children's Books.

———. 1999. *Pigs*. New York: Holiday House.

Hutchins, Pat. *Rosie's walk*. 1968. New York: Simon and Schuster Children's Books.

Microsoft Corporation. Microsoft Encarta 98.

Miller, Sara Swan. 2000. *A true book: Pigs*. New York: Children's Press/Grolier.

Simon, Carly, and David Delamare. 1997. *Midnight farm*. New York: Simon and Schuster Children's Books.

Thomson, Ruth. 1978. *Understanding farm animals*. London: Usborne Publishing.

Theme Kit 4

Caps for Sale

You will like the story Caps for Sale; it has a big surprise.
See what happens when the peddler sits and shuts his eyes.

Peddlers are people who roam up and down the street,
Trying to sell wares to everyone they meet.

What do the peddlers sell? How do they carry their wares?
Pots and pans, hats and caps, and even kitchen chairs!

Peddlers carry goods on their back, or push them in a cart;
This peddler has another idea that he thinks is real smart!

After you hear the story, act it out and pretend
That you are the peddler or his silly monkey friends!

Theme Tree

Monkeys
natural habitat
monkeys in zoos
monkeys at the circus
food
lifestyle

Hats
caps
jockey cap
sports cap
monkey cap (small pillbox
    hat with chin strap)
graduation cap
work hats
artist beret
construction
cowboy/girl hat
helmets
fancy hats
special event hats
top hat

Peddlers
city shopping and country
    shopping
shopping before there was
    transportation
sales people
ways to shop
    mall
    open air markets
    farmer's markets
    Internet shopping

**How do people
carry things?**
baskets on heads
in shopping bags
in backpacks
on carts
on bicycles
on mules
on dogsleds

Feelings
peddler is hungry—no money
    for lunch
how to help people who have
    no money for food—soup
    kitchens
peddler is tired—takes nap
peddler is angry—shakes finger
peddler is more angry—raises
    voice, stamps foot
peddler is super angry—stomps
    both feet, throws hat

Questions for discussion
Did you ever take anything that
    did not belong to you?
Did anyone ever take something
    from you without asking?
What do you do when you are
    angry?
Do you have any ideas for how
    the peddler could have gotten
    his hats back?

Introduction

Caps for Sale is the book that made me feel like a master preschool teacher! It worked like magic every time. Whether it was my three-year-old class, the early intervention program, or my kindergarten group, the children were enchanted by the simple tale and loved to act it out.

Treat your children to this special book and watch the fun unfold. If you think you have your hands full now, wait until you have a room full of monkeys! It's all in a day's work.

Kit Contents

Several copies of the book *Caps for Sale,* so that there's no need to fight over one copy

A selection of stories about monkeys

***Curious George* (Rey)**

***Five Little Monkeys Jumping on the Bed* (Christelow)**

***Five Little Monkeys with Nothing to Do* (Christelow)**

***Little Gorilla* (Bornstein)**—Will an adorable baby gorilla still get love and attention when he grows up to be a big ape?

***Gorillas: Gentle Giants of the Forest: A Step 2 Book* (Milton)**

***The Monkey and the Crocodile: A Jataka tale from India* (Galdone)**

***The Hatseller and the Monkeys* (Diakité)**—BaMusa is the hatseller in this vividly illustrated West African version of *Caps for Sale.*

***I Am a Little Monkey* (Crozat)**—Watch this monkey to learn how to collect ants and carry out other monkey business.

***So Say the Little Monkeys* (Laan)**—Travel deep into the rain forest and see some playful monkeys learn a wet and cold lesson.

Stories about hats

***Miss Fannie's Hat* (Karon)**—Almost 100 years old, Miss Fannie donates her favorite hat to a good cause.

***The 500 Hats of Bartholomew Cubbins* (Seuss)**

Aunt Flossie's Hats (and Crab Cakes Later) **(Howard)**—Every hat comes with a story; what's yours?

The Hat **(Brett)**—Illustrator/storyteller Jan Brett introduces Hedgie the hedgehog, who starts a trend among his barnyard friends.

Old Hat, New Hat **(Berenstain)**—A great book for a new reader.

Commercial products

set of community worker hats

Barrel of Monkeys game

Jenga block-balancing game

Tree Blocks toy (see appendix 2)

Play props

If you use real hats, consider sanitation. To avoid spreading lice, some programs use disposable shower caps or hospital surgical caps to place on the child's head before using a hat.

hats (encourage children to bring their own)

monkey puppets

a safe way for children to be elevated as if in a tree; consider allowing them to sit on a low table

Signs to post

BEWARE—MONKEYS IN TREES

Labels on sorting baskets: CHECKED CAPS, GRAY CAPS, BROWN CAPS, BLUE CAPS, RED CAPS

COUNTRY—THIS WAY (with an arrow)

CITY—THIS WAY (with an arrow)

Other materials

hats from workers, hats from other countries, special event hats, and more (if you are concerned about sanitation, reserve these for display only)

Facts about Monkeys

- Monkeys are primates. They are warm-blooded, have fur, and feed their own babies.

- Primates have large brains and are very intelligent.

- Primates have hands, not claws, and are very adept at climbing.

- The primate group includes 158 species of monkeys, 14 apes, and 61 prosimians (ancient primates living mostly on Madagascar Island).

- Most primates live together in groups of multiple families.

- Primates are good parents. The extended family helps to care for the babies.

- Grooming is common among primates; they groom each other and themselves meticulously.

- Monkeys live in trees and eat leaves, fruit, and insects.

Source: Primate Primer: Pictures and Information about Monkeys and Apes, www.animaltime.net/primates.

Family Involvement

One way to include families in your program is to write letters. I think it is respectful to children if we include them in the process. At the very least, be sure children know *exactly* what the letter that is being sent home says, and choose a greeting that includes all the people living in a child's home (mom, dad, grandma, big sister, and so on). Other children might choose to fill in Dear _____ and sign their own names.

Dear _____,

We are working on a theme based on a favorite story. The story is called *Caps for Sale.* It's about a peddler, the caps he sells, and a bunch of monkeys. When you come into my room (child care), would you add your ideas to the Theme Tree?

Do you have any of the following materials to loan or give to our class (child care) to help us enjoy this theme?

- special hats
- work hats
- play hats
- dress-up hats

Here are some activities we will be doing:

- sorting and counting hats
- learning about the people who wear the hats
- acting out the story
- learning how to express anger
- identifying fabrics by pattern: stripes, checks, plaid, polka dots

Get ready to ask me these questions at the end of this unit of study:

- What should you do if someone takes something from you and they won't give it back?
- The peddler carried his hats on his head; what are some other ways people carry things from place to place?
- What kind of hat is your favorite?

Thanks for all your help.

Your daughter (son),

Ready, Set, Go!

Daily routines

Arrival

Invite children to wear hats to school on a designated day.

Breakfast

Serve bananas, of course!

Circle

Read the poem and then the book. On another circle day, make a K-W-L chart about monkeys. (What do children *Know* about monkeys, what do they *Want* to know, and what have they *Learned?*)

Free choice

See the interest areas described below.

Outdoor play

You will need to set limits as to where the "monkeys" can pretend to be in the "trees."

Small group time

Make pretend hats from fabric using the colors and patterns of the peddlers hats. Children can sort them, count them, and make patterns.

Broaden your study to another kind of "caps," and collect all kinds of bottle caps. See how many shoeboxes you can fill with caps. They are fun for sorting, counting, and seriating from smallest to largest. If you have enough of one kind, you can put matching stickers on the inside and make a concentration game (make about ten pairs of matching caps).

Rest time

Try a special rest time, peddler-style, outside under a tree. This will not replace nap time; do it as a special activity one morning.

Interest areas

Dramatic play

- Vary the story a little. Tell the children that this week the peddler is selling bracelets. What will the monkeys do? Try scarves, socks, books.

Table activities

- Play matching games.
- Provide puzzles with a rain forest theme.

Art and projects

- Read *Curious George Rides a Bike;* follow his instructions for making a newspaper boat and a newspaper hat.

Library

- See the list of books in Kit Contents.

New discoveries

- Learn about balance, using Jenga-brand blocks or Tree Blocks.

Writing center

- Prepare cutouts of monkeys. Each child can select a monkey and give it a name. They can be made into stick puppets.

Music and movement

- Show the children photographs of monkeys in natural settings and, if possible, a clip from a nature video showing monkeys. Before children try to move like monkeys, they should observe them in motion. Dramatize children sneaking up monkey-style to the peddler to steal his hats one by one.
- Play a mimic game similar to Simon Says, just like the monkeys did in the story.

Activity Ideas

Peddler play

Talk to children about setting up a store to sell wares. What would they like to sell (for pretend)? Agree on prices for the items. Children can announce the price whenever a customer (another child) comes by: "Books, books for sale, fifty cents a book."

Hide a hat

One child designated as "monkey" hides a hat in the room, while the "peddler" waits outside. All the other "monkeys" take turns giving hints to the "peddler" to help him find the hat. Help children use these position words in their hints: *near, under, over, next to, on,* and so on.

Art museum hat hunt

This can be at the museum, or you can bring the museum into the classroom. Focus on hats: How many hats can they find in paintings, on sculptures, and in other art forms? If you do this activity at home or at school, use art pictures from calendars or postcards (available at museum gift shops). Set up the room like a museum. Post pictures on all the walls. String a line a couple feet from the walls to show the children the path they should walk to view the art. How many pictures show people wearing hats? Which is the fanciest, the simplest, the funniest?

Resources

Berenstain, Stan, and Jan Berenstain. 1970. *Old hat, new hat.* New York: Random House.

Bornstein, Ruth. 2000. *Little gorilla.* New York: Houghton Mifflin.

Brett, Jan. 1997. *The hat.* New York: Putnam.

Christelow, Eileen. 1996. *Five little monkeys with nothing to do.* New York: Houghton Mifflin.

———. 1998. *Five little monkeys jumping on the bed.* New York: Houghton Mifflin.

Crozat, Francois. 1991. *I am a little monkey.* New York: Scholastic.

Diakité, Baba Wagué. 1999. *The hatseller and the monkeys.* New York: Scholastic.

Galdone, Paul. 1997. *The monkey and the crocodile: A Jataka tale from India.* New York: Houghton Mifflin.

Howard, Elizabeth. 1995. *Aunt Flossie's hats (and crab cakes later).* New York: Houghton Mifflin.

Karon, Jan. 2001. *Miss Fannie's hat.* New York: Penguin Putnam Books for Young Readers.

Laan, Nancy Van. 1998. *So say the little monkeys.* New York: Simon and Schuster Children's Books.

Milton, Joyce. 1997. *Gorillas: Gentle giants of the forest.* New York: Random House.

Morris, Ann. 1989. *Hats, hats, hats.* New York: Lothrop, Lee & Shepard Books.

Rey, H. A. 1973. *Curious George.* Boston: Houghton Mifflin.

———. 1973. *Curious George rides a bike.* Boston: Houghton Mifflin.

Seuss, Dr. 1976. *The 500 hats of Bartholomew Cubbins.* New York: Random House.

Slobodkina, Esphyr. 1940. *Caps for sale.* New York: W. R. Scott.

The Three Billy Goats Gruff

*What would you do if you were taking a stroll
across a bridge, and you met a mean troll?*

*This story's about three billy goats named Gruff
Who met a troll acting mean and tough!*

*This troll didn't have a name, or a home of his own,
He lived under a bridge that was built from stone.*

*He was tired and hungry when the goats came near;
Trip Trap! Trip Trap! was all he could hear.*

*"Who's that tramping on my bridge!" he exclaimed.
"It is I—little billy goat Gruff is my name."*

*The troll shouted he wanted a goat to eat;
The goat tricked him and promised a bigger treat.*

*The middle billy goat said, "Wait for big brother Gruff."
The troll shouted louder and huffed and puffed.*

*Then the big goat got mad and hurt the troll.
It's time they both learned some self-control!*

*What should the troll do? What can the goat say?
Can you solve their problems in a peaceful way?*

Theme Tree

Goats
on a farm
in the wild
as domesticated animals raised
  for their hair
physical characteristics
new words: hooves, hollow
  horns, udder

Trolls
monsters
real/make-believe
fears
problem solving

Sounds
Predict loud and quiet "trip
  trap" sounds for big and
  small goat.
other loud and soft sounds

Geography words
mountain
hill
river
valley
meadow

Bridges
types of bridges
people and bridges:
  Who designs bridges?
  Who builds bridges?
  Who paints bridges?
  Who operates bridges?
  Who collects tolls?

Siblings
Three Billy Goats Gruff were
brothers. Record number
and gender of siblings of
children in your group.

Introduction

Why do children, year after year, telling upon telling, maintain a fascination with the story of The Three Billy Goats Gruff? This story, first translated into English from Norwegian in 1859, is retold by countless authors in many languages.

What are the elements that make it so popular? Simplicity is one: the plot is so simple that even a very young child can understand it. Predictability is another: children quickly begin to anticipate the ending. The story is timeless: the animal characters, the country setting, and the mean troll could exist anytime, anywhere. It addresses our fears. As long as there are children, there will be fears to contend with. Children need opportunities to explore their fears in a safe way, from the monster under the bed to the strict substitute teacher. A story with a mean, scary troll allows children to learn about facing fear, but at a safe distance. And the story has a happy ending, at least from the goats' perspective. We will explore the story from the troll's point of view and see if we can create an even happier ending.

Many early childhood educators would not advocate the use of a story where violence offers a solution. Well, I agree that violence is not a solution, but I'm not convinced we should censor classic stories that portray violence this way. Let's learn from our children. If they want to listen to and reenact this tale over and over, they have something to gain from it. Let this be a way to open dialogue on peaceful problem solving.

You and the children will learn a lot about goats through this theme kit. Some of the facts belie what the story implies. In fact, goats do not eat much grass. They prefer plants, roots, nuts, berries, and shrubbery (Miller 2000, 20–21). The children might want to change the story to make it more accurate!

The Three Billy Goats Gruff story also gives us an opportunity to take a closer look at bridges. Bridges connect people, places, and things all over the world. Bridges have been around for thousands of years and have played an enormous role in the history of our world. Once I started researching bridges, I saw the potential for a theme kit about bridges. As they say, we can cross that bridge when we come to it!

Kit Contents

A selection of Three Billy Goats Gruff stories

***The Three Billy Goats Gruff* (Galdone)**—In this traditional retelling, the language used as the troll is overthrown is harsher than in some versions: the big billy goat "butted" and "trampled" him.

***The Three Billy Goats Gruff* (Stevens)**—I like the language, the humor, and the illustrations in this version.

***The Truth about Three Billy Goats Gruff* (Otfinoski)**—This tale is told by Tobias T. Troll, the misunderstood toll troll whose story makes a great read-aloud while settling down for nap. There's more text than in most versions.

***The Gruff Brothers* (Hooks)**—Part of the Bank Street Ready-to-Read series, this version uses a rebus style, which is perfect for one-on-one reading with early readers. Descriptive language and the addition of a fox, a snake, a sheep, a duck, and a bird enrich the story.

***The Three Billy Goats Gruff* (Finch)**—The illustrations are a colorful, creative treat that might stimulate some interesting art in your class. This traditional retelling ends when the big goat "picked up his hooves and kicked the troll into the middle of next week!"

Books about bridges

***New True Book of Bridges* (Carlisle)**—Don't be fooled by the 1965 publication date; this book is full of fascinating, relevant information.

***Bridges* (Baxter)**—This book covers the topic brilliantly. Some of the information is advanced for young children, but it's an excellent and entertaining resource. It includes science experiments to try in class.

***Bridges Are to Cross* (Sturges)**—Utilizing great visuals for the young viewer, this book features a worldwide history tour of bridges with a simple statement of purpose for each one.

***Make It Work! Building* (Haslam)**—Here's an opportunity to engage some talented parents. There are instructions to make model drawbridges, keystone bridges, aqueducts, and other types of bridges. A parent might enjoy the challenge; the children will love the results.

***Bridges Connect* (Hill)**—This book offers a perfect introduction to bridges. There's even a reference to The Three Billy Goats Gruff and The Three Little Pigs.

Books about goats and trolls

***Ogres! Ogres! Ogres! A Feasting Frenzy from A to Z* (Heller)**—Ogres, very similar to trolls in physical characteristics, have some unique names and eating habits in this joyously illustrated book.

***The Goat in the Rug* (Blood and Link)**—This most delightful story is essential to complement this theme kit. Geraldine generously gives her hair to Glenmae, a Navajo woman, to weave a rug. Other peoples who weave rugs from goat hair include the Maya and the Inca.

***The Toll-Bridge Troll* (Wolff)**—Riddles and tricks win over the troll who harasses a young boy on his way to school.

***Trouble with Trolls* (Brett)**—In Jan Brett's vibrant illustrations, we meet a band of trolls who get outwitted by a little girl.

***700 Kids on Grandpa's Farm* (Morris)**—The photos tell the whole story, from raising goats to making and selling cheese.

***Beatrice's Goat* (McBrier)**—Goats earn some real status here: Hillary Rodham Clinton wrote the afterword. The book celebrates Heifer Project International, which provides animals to help families build better lives through self-reliance. In western Uganda, young Beatrice receives the gift of a goat. Her goat, Mugisa (means "luck"), brings her family enough milk for their own nourishment and extra to sell, so that she can afford to go to the village school. The goat was a gift to Beatrice; this story is a gift to us. A heartwarming story, beautifully told and illustrated.

***Gregory the Terrible Eater* (Sharmat)**—This is one of a very few fictional picture books to feature a goat. Although a goat's appetite is not accurately depicted, it will stimulate some discussion on nutrition.

Play props

set of plastic or wood goats for block area (may need extra sets to get three goats)

wicker window shade or beach mat to serve as a "bridge"

blue shower curtain, cloth, or plastic to represent water under the bridge

drum or other small instruments for "trip trap" sound effects

tap shoes or leather-soled shoes for "trip trap" sound effects

goatee or beard from costume

nesting cups or other manipulative items representing "small to big"

sets of soft plastic animals in different sizes

white apron and white rubber boots to wear in "creamery"

pictures of famous bridges

Commercial products

See appendix 2 for information on how to find products.

Story Teller felt pieces and mounted background scene; set of billy goat soft masks

ChildWood Magnets magnetic goats, troll, and scenery

Folkmanis goat puppet, realistic hand puppet

All Aboard Runaway Train—Classic Tunes and Tales to Grow Up With from Jasmine Music (musical narration of the story on cassette)

Toano Toy Works farm scene cube puzzle; wooden blocks fit together to make a bucolic farm scene; includes image of billy goats

Learning Materials Workshop Arcobaleno set of curved blocks presented as a puzzle and suitable for bridge and tunnel building

Signs to post

GOAT MILK FOR SALE

DANGER: MEAN TROLL

FRESH GRASS—THIS WAY!

Other materials

balance beam or wood planks

tunnel (we go over a bridge, through a tunnel)

scale

samples of yarn or clothing from goat hair: mohair, angora

children's lap loom

corn, oats, barley, soybeans, hay—foods that goats eat (in addition to sweet grass from the hillside)

Peruvian rattle made of goat hooves

cow hooves (available in pet supply stores, for dogs to chew on)

Facts about Goats

- A goat has hooves (a hard covering of the toes) and hollow horns.
- Goats' pupils are rectangular, not round like human pupils.
- Goats are closely related to sheep. Sheep have dense wool; goats have hair.
- Male goats are known commonly as billy goats, or bucks, and have beards.
- Female goats are sometimes referred to as nanny goats, or does.
- Young goats are called kids.
- The natural habitat for goats is mountainous country. They are highly adept at leaping from rock to rock.
- There are more than 200 breeds of goats.
- Goats eat grass and branches and leaves of shrubs.
- Goats are raised in large numbers in the United States for their milk and meat.
- More people get their milk from goats than from cows, worldwide. Goats give less milk than cows (approximately four quarts of milk a day), which works well for people who do not have refrigeration.
- Goat manure makes fantastic fertilizer to support vegetable crops.
- Some people have goats as outdoor pets.
- Other parts of the goat are used to make leather, and the fur pelts are used for rugs.
- Some types of goats are raised for their hair. An angora goat produces long, silky hair called mohair, used to make yarn and fabric.

Sources: Microsoft Encarta 98, Microsoft Corporation; Miller, Sara Swan, *Goats* (New York: Children's Press, 2000); Heifer Project International.

Family Involvement

One way to include families in your program is to write letters. I think it is respectful to children if we include them in the process. At the very least, be sure children know exactly what the letter that is being sent home says, and choose a greeting that includes all the people living in a child's home (mom, dad, grandma, big sister, and so on). Other children might choose to fill in Dear _____ and sign their own names.

Dear _____,

We are working on a theme based on a favorite story. The story is called "The Three Billy Goats Gruff." It's about three billy goats who want to cross a bridge to get to the fresh grass and a mean troll who blocks their way. When you come into my room, would you add your ideas to the Theme Tree?

Do you have any of these materials to loan or give to our class (child care) to help us enjoy this theme?

- clothing or yarn made from mohair or angora
- tap shoes
- drum

Here are some activities we will be doing:

- dramatizing the story
- brainstorming peaceful solutions to the problem the goats face
- growing grass
- exploring other examples of small, medium, big (like the goats)
- building bridges

Get ready to ask me these questions at the end of this unit of study:

- Why are there bridges?
- How does a drawbridge work?
- Do you think the billy goats did the right thing by throwing the troll off the bridge? How could they have solved their problem peacefully?
- What do we get from goats?

Thanks for all your help.

Your daughter (son),

Ready, Set, Go!

Daily routines

Arrival

Welcome the children with your portable mat "bridge" at the door. Invite children to trip-trap over it and announce their arrival. Of course, any accompanying grown-ups are welcome to be big billy goats.

Breakfast

Goats like to eat nuts and berries. Have an assortment for children to add to their cereal. (Be attentive to nut or berry allergies.)

Circle

Introduce topic by reading the poem or one of the traditional goat tales.

Free choice

See interest areas described below.

Outdoor play

If the story has captured the children's interest, they will find ways to enact it outdoors.

Small group time

Sort items by size. Offer weaving activities.

Lunch

Offer goat milk.

Rest time

Some people count sheep to fall asleep; try counting goats out loud as a group. While the lights are on, tell children to count together as high as they can until the lights go out. Time for all "kids" to go to sleep!

Interest Areas

Blocks and building

- Display pictures of bridges.
- Add boats, trains, and cars as play props for bridges.
- Post pictures of mountains; provide commercial egg cartons that children can pile up like the rocks goats like to leap on.

Dramatic play

- Set up a bridge over water.
- Use drum or other props for sound of "trip trapping."
- See goat masks in Kit Contents.

Manipulative and math center

- Offer a set of curved blocks, such as Arcobaleno blocks, for bridge and tunnel building. (See the Learning Materials Workshop entry in appendix 2 for these blocks.)
- Sequence nesting cups from small to large.
- Build small bridges with tongue depressors or frozen-dessert sticks.

Art and projects

- Make stick puppets or finger puppets using characters from the story.

Sensory station

- Provide samples of angora and mohair.
- Invite a goat to school—check with local dairy farms and 4-H clubs.

Library

- See the list of books in Kit Contents.

New discoveries

- Grow grass: Fill a container, such as a clay pot saucer, with potting soil. Moisten the soil. Cover the entire surface lightly with grass seed (winter rye seed germinates quickly). Press the seeds in firmly. Lightly water. Wrap the entire container with plastic wrap. Keep in a sunny location. You should see results in a week!

Writing center

- Display flannelboard and story pieces so children can retell the story in their own words. Stories can be transcribed on paper.

Music and movement

- Listen to the story on tape or CD.
- Practice making "trip trapping" sounds rhythmically on a drum.

Activity ideas

Measure up!

This is a great time to bring out the measuring tools and graph children's sizes. You can graph children from small to large based on shoe size, height, and weight. Parents might be willing to participate in the shoe-size graph. After the graphs are complete, use your results to name people using ordinal numbers: "If we were billy goats trying to cross the bridge, who would go first, second, third, and so on?" Be attuned to sensitivities about differences that might arise from this activity; think of measurements that would put children in different size orders.

Story mapping

Make magnet pieces by gluing images onto pasteboard and attaching to magnetic tape. The pieces should represent three goats of different sizes, a bridge, a hillside with flowers and grass, and a troll. Divide a cookie sheet or magnetic board into four parts. Label the sections with the words *Who? Where? When?* and *Why?* Show children how to place magnets in the appropriate quadrants based on these questions:

- Who are the characters in this story?
- Where did the troll live?
- When (season) did this story take place?
- Why was there a problem? Which character belongs here?

The quadrants could also be labeled 1 to 4, and children could retell the story sequentially.
(This idea was adapted from www.childwoodmagnets.com.)

Tasting party

Have different milk samples available. Offer cow's milk in skim, 1 percent, 2 percent, and whole, and include goat's milk. You can also offer soy milk. Make a graph of "favorite type of milk." You can do a similar activity with goat cheese versus cow's-milk cheeses. Be prepared for lots of turned-up noses. Goat cheese has a strong taste and odor; the odor is similar to the smell of a goat.

Try this recipe:

Sherbet

    1 quart goat's milk
    1 cup sugar
    ½ cup corn syrup
    Juice of 3 lemons
    Pinch of salt

Mix the milk, sugar, corn syrup, and salt together. Pour it into a loaf pan. Put it in the freezer. When it's partly frozen, stir in the lemon juice. Stir the mixture twice more while it's freezing to make it smoother. It should be ready in about two hours.

(Miller 2000, 42)

New stories

- Display other play animals, besides goats, in sets of three. Ask children what the title of the story would be if these animals were the characters instead of the goats: pigs, horses, mice (or other animals you choose). What would motivate these animals to cross the bridge? In what other ways would the story change?

- Read *The Truth about Three Billy Goats Gruff*. What did the children like about the troll in this story? How would they describe the goats' behavior? Try dramatizing the classic version of the story with a nice, innocent troll and three mean, ugly goats.

No trolls; tolls!

We don't have trolls protecting our bridges, we have toll collectors. What is a toll? Why do we pay tolls? Learn all you can about toll collectors. Set up a toll collection booth in your classroom or home. Children can decide how much to charge for each person, vehicle, or animal that crosses the bridge. Does a car pay as much as a truck? Should a mouse pay as much as an elephant?

Resources

Baxter, Nicola. 2000. *Topic books: Bridges.* New York: Franklin Watts/Grolier Publishing.

Blood, Charles, and Martin Link. 1988. *The goat in the rug.* New York: Simon and Schuster.

Carlisle, Norman, and Madelyn Carlisle. 1965. *New true book of bridges.* Chicago: Children's Press.

Finch, Mary. 2001. *The three billy goats Gruff.* New York: Barefoot Books.

Galdone, Paul. 1973. *The three billy goats Gruff.* New York: Clarion Books.

———. 1996. *Los tres chivitos Gruff.* New York: Lectorum Publications.

Haslam, Andrew. 1994. *Make it work! Building.* Chicago: World Book, Inc.

Heller, Nicholas. 1999. *Ogres! Ogres! Ogres! A feasting frenzy from A to Z.* New York: Greenwillow Press.

Hill, Lee Sullivan. 1997. *Bridges connect.* Minneapolis: Carolrhoda Books.

Hooks, William H. 1997. *The Gruff Brothers.* Milwaukee: Gareth Stevens Publishing.

McBrier, Page. *Beatrice's goat.* 2001. New York: Atheneum.

Miller, Sara Swan. 2000. *Goats.* New York: Children's Press.

Morris, Ann. 1994. *700 kids on Grandpa's farm.* New York: Dutton Children's Books.

Otfinoski, Steven. 1994. *The truth about three billy goats Gruff.* Mahwah, N.J.: Whistlestop/Troll Associates.

Sharmat, Mitchell. 1980. *Gregory, the terrible eater.* New York: Scholastic Inc.

Stevens, Janet. 1987. *The three billy goats Gruff.* San Diego: Harcourt Brace Jovanovich.

Sturges, Philemon. 1998. *Bridges are to cross.* New York: G. P. Putnam.

Wolff, Patricia Rae. 1995. *The toll-bridge troll.* San Diego: Browndeer Press.

Theme Kit 6

Buttons

Buttons, buttons everywhere, look around now:
If you have some on your clothes, stand up and take a bow.

Sometimes round and sometimes square, any kind of shape,
Buttons hold your clothes together better than tape!

Sometimes friends lose buttons—like Corduroy the bear.
Sometimes they get found by looking here and there.

Wait, I think I just found one that I like best:
It's my belly button, here, under my chest.

Then there are telephone and television buttons, and many, many more;
Can we make a list of buttons to find when we explore?

We'll collect them, sort them, and count from one to ten,
Make patterns, pictures, button soup—the fun might never end!

Theme Tree

Sewing
sewing machine
Teachers make button holes.

Colors
How many different colors of buttons
can you find? Look for light to dark
shades of each color.
matching colors

Patterns
Use buttons to make patterns.

Counting
Estimate how many in a button jar.
count and graph
Make gingerbread kids—give them
raisin buttons.
Count the buttons on a wedding gown.

Shapes
Name the shapes.
Match shapes.

Other buttons
elevator buttons
belly buttons
telephone buttons
campaign or advertising
buttons
a switch that you push—
such as a doorbell, car
radio button, push-
button lock on a door
knob, vending machine
Identify toys at school
and at home that have
buttons.

**Clothes vocabulary
(clothes that may
have buttons)**
pants
shirts
shirtsleeves
dress
skirt
shorts
pajamas
robe
coat
raincoat
sweater
jacket

Jewelry
Make button rings, necklaces,
bracelets, pins.

**Natural materials (that
become buttons)**
Collect buttons, for
display only, made of
these materials:
sand—glass
tree—wood
oyster—shell
clay—porcelain
bamboo
bone

Self-help skills
button
zip
Open and close Velcro.
Tie a knot or a bow.
snap

Introduction

Why a button kit? Well, you'd have to know me to understand. I like collecting affordable and aesthetically pleasing items, including buttons. I love their simplicity, practicality, and endless variations. I think they're perfect for good old-fashioned fun and exploration.

If you love history, art, collecting, or jewelry, you'll love the button theme too. Buttons have been made popular by various cultures and by kings, queens, and American presidents. Every famous period of art is reflected in a style of buttons. Men and women of seventeenth-century Europe wore buttons for show like fine jewelry. Your time will be well spent garnering enthusiasm for buttons in your class.

As writer Hajo Bücken said, "The only rule where buttons are concerned is that they should not be used solely for the purpose of buttoning up (Bücken 1995, 7)!" This is one theme that probably won't dominate your dramatic play area. This theme kit will lend itself to a variety of language and manipulative math activities, craft projects, and creative expression.

This may be the only theme kit that comes with a serious safety disclaimer. Do not use buttons with children under age three or with children who still put objects in their mouths.

Kit Contents

A selection of button stories

The Button Box **(Reid)**—This book, also available in Spanish (*La caja de los botones*) has a young boy, pictured on the front cover, looking pensively at a tin of buttons that belongs to his grandma. A wonderful way to introduce this new topic.

Button Soup **(Orgel)**—You've heard of "Stone Soup;" well, this is the urban version. Used as an easy reader, *Button Soup* tells the story of Rag-Tag Meg and friend Mandy, who concoct this delectable meal.

Frog and Toad Are Friends **(Lobel)**—One of the stories, "Lost Button," tells as much about friendship as it does about buttons and their many attributes.

Corduroy **(Freeman)**—No child should graduate from preschool without being introduced to Lisa and her bear friend, Corduroy. The adventures of a button—and love—lost and then found have never been better told.

Button, Button, Who's Got the Button? 101 Button Games (Bücken)—You'll never look at a button quite the same way after you read 101 game ideas using buttons. There's a wide age range addressed through these activities. Adapt them to meet your needs.

Buttons Buttons (Williams)—A simplistic, colorful paperback, this book is part of a science series called Learn to Read, Read to Learn.

Blue's Buttons (Johnson)—I'm not fond of commercialized books, but button beggars can't be choosers. There are not that many button books around. This works well with the youngest among us!

I Like Your Buttons! (Lamstein)—The power of a compliment is the focus of this delightful picture book; starting with the appeal of the teacher's large, glittery buttons is a bonus!

Button Crafts (Holtschlag)—This would be a good book to send home with a container of buttons. Let the child and family members choose a project.

Buttons (Cole)—This original, whimsical story is more of a fairy tale with exaggerated and traditional gender roles. Its appeal is that this tale was built upon buttons!

The Button Blanket: An Activity Book (McNutt)—One in a series of books about Northwest Coast Indian art, this title includes a short story with realistic black-and-white line drawings of a young girl, Ann, preparing for her family's potlatch celebration. Ann counts out 300 buttons to add to the special blanket she will wear at the festival.

Joseph Had a Little Overcoat (Taback)—I think the moral of this story, "You can always make something out of nothing," is what thematic teaching is all about. You're only limited by your imagination.

Tasty Baby Belly Buttons (Sierra)—This is a variation of a famous Japanese folktale with a heroine, the melon princess. Like American folktales, this has some monster-like characters, some references to violence, and some fun words similar to *fee-fi-fo-fum!*

Play props

dress-up clothes with a variety of buttons

uniforms (add shiny metal buttons to standard jackets)

cooking pot (like the one in *Button Soup*)

stuffed bears to represent Corduroy (multiples are a good idea)

materials for beginning sewing projects:

> large plastic needles
> berry baskets
> yarn
> containers for sorting buttons
> buttons, the more the merrier; see you at the yard sales!

Other materials

worker uniforms

The Original Buttoneer (attaches buttons without sewing—As on TV Products in appendix 2)

ButtonQuick (for button repairs)

clothing from other time periods (may or may not have button fasteners)

Facts about Buttons

- Ancient Greeks used buttons held by loops to fasten their tunics.
- Buttonholes were invented in the thirteenth century, making the use of buttons much more popular.
- In thirteenth-century Europe, kings wore buttons to show their wealth and importance. One king covered his suit with 13,600 buttons.
- Buttons have been made from gold, silver, ivory, bone, wood, steel, ceramic, glass, seashells, nuts, deer antlers, and, most recently, plastic.
- Paul Revere made the first silver buttons.
- Buttons come in a variety of colors, shapes, materials, sizes, textures; some have shanks instead of holes.
- Some people bite on a button to see if it's made from plastic or seashell.
- Buttons are very popular to collect and can be worth a lot of money.
- The tip of a rattlesnake's rattle is called a button.
- The zipper supplanted the popularity of buttons for fastening clothes in the early 1900s.

Sources: Microsoft Encarta 98, Microsoft Corporation; *Compton's Encyclopedia* (Chicago: Compton's, 1990); *Encyclopaedia Britannica* (Chicago: Encyclopaedia Britannica, Inc., n.d.)

Family Involvement

One way to include families in your program is to write letters. I think it is respectful to children if we include them in the process. At the very least, be sure children know exactly what the letter that is being sent home says, and choose a greeting that includes all the people living in a child's home (mom, dad, grandma, big sister, and so on). Other children might choose to fill in Dear _____ and sign their own names.

Dear _____,

We are learning about buttons in my class. When you come into my room (child care), would you add your ideas to the Button Theme Tree? Can you help me look around our home for some buttons to bring to preschool? We need a variety of buttons for our Button Museum.

Here are some activities we will be doing:

- counting and sorting by color, shape, and size
- collecting (Can we fill our button jar?)
- problem solving to help story characters find their lost buttons
- sewing
- playing button games
- creating art projects

Get ready to ask me these questions at the end of this unit of study:

- What letter does the word *button* begin with?
- What is a shank?
- Tell me what the button on my shirt is made from.

Thanks for all your help.

Your daughter (son),

Ready, Set, Go!

Daily routines

Arrival

Children announce their arrival each day by choosing buttons from the "welcome button box." Each child puts the "welcome button" in a clear snack-size plastic bag (which has been secured to the child's cubbie) or on a board next to the child's name. At the end of the week, each child counts the buttons collected.

Circle

Introduce the topic by reading a book from Kit Contents list; or by playing Button, Button, Who's Got the Button?; or by having children stand when you describe buttons they're wearing. Call out colors, shapes, sizes, textures, and pattern descriptions.

Free choice

See the interest areas described below.

Outdoor play

Hide buttons in the play area.

Small group time

Sort buttons.

Lunch

Hide buttons under someone's placemat or plate each day. Whoever has the hidden button gets a special lunchtime job.

Interest areas

Blocks and building

- Provide a box of buttons, and let the children's imaginations take charge. Will the buttons become wheels? architectural details? windows for buildings?

Dramatic play

- See dress-up items listed in Kit Contents.

Table activities

- Provide bowls of buttons with sorting containers. The best selection of containers is usually at craft or large home improvement/hardware stores. The more compartments, the better. (I use a plastic storage unit with twelve to sixteen compartments that is made for hardware.)
- Make button patterns: Start with a simple three-part repeating pattern on a strip of oaktag, and encourage children to continue the pattern. Try covering the strip of oaktag with self-adhesive paper and then add a top layer, sticky-side up—buttons will easily attach and are removable.
- Try a variation of the previous activity. Use a magnetic board (or cookie sheet) and pieces of magnetic tape adhered to the back of each button.

Art and projects

- Provide containers of buttons and other fabric-related collage materials such as fabric scraps, snaps, zippers, spools, and so on.

Sensory station

- Put a variety of buttons in the sand or water table with scoop and sifters.
- Fill a sensory bag with textured buttons; children look at and feel one button, then reach into the bag and use their sense of touch to find its match.

Library

- See the list of books in Kit Contents.

New discoveries

- Collect natural materials and buttons made from the raw materials; compare other products made from the same material as the buttons.

  metal—silverware, tools, hubcap
  plastic—toys, lunchbox
  glass (with supervision only)—drinking glass, vase, mirror
  clay—flower pot, dishes

Writing center

- Pre-glue buttons on paper in a random design (one or more per page); encourage the child to draw a picture that incorporates the buttons and to dictate a matching sentence or story.

Music and movement

Maybe I'm showing my age, but I can't resist the idea of young children singing the Frank Sinatra tune "Button Up Your Overcoat." See complete lyrics at the Heptune Lyrics Web site (see appendix 2). If you're not sure of the tune, just ask anyone over fifty!

Activity ideas

Button museum

Have the children ever visited a museum? Spend some time talking about what they know and filling in the unknowns. Acquaint them with the incredible array of museums that exist, including museums featuring art, science, history, prehistoric animals, seashells, lace, bicycles, baseball, space, and cars.

People visit museums to learn new information, to be entertained, and to stimulate new interests. What could you include in a Button Museum so that friends, schoolmates, and family members would like to come?

Maybe the admission ticket to your museum would be a button. Could you have a museum gift shop of items made from buttons?

Sewing buttons

This activity requires individualized supervision. Cut two squares (about 8 inches to 10 inches square) per child from felt, burlap, or other loosely woven fabric. Make buttonholes in the centers of half of the squares, ideally with a sewing machine (but simply cutting a slit will do in a pinch). Give the other squares to the children and help them choose a button to sew in the center of each square.

Button poems

This activity works best one-on-one or with a small group of children. Ask the children to choose buttons from the button box for the poems they are going to write. Brainstorm a list of images that come to mind when they look at their buttons. Generate a list of ideas by asking the children, "What does your button look like? What does this button make you think of? What is round like this button? What is red and round like this button?"

Let each child choose words from the list for their poems. The first two lines of a poem can be, "The _____ is like a button./ I like it the very best."

Next ask each child to tell you at least three details about the button. Think of color, shape, size, texture, brightness, and so on.

Fill in the next two lines: "It's _____, _____, and _____,/ Prettier than all the rest."

Button creations

Buttons and pipe cleaners make perfect partners. Use long pipe cleaners and a variety of buttons, some with holes and some with shanks. The children can create button jewelry.

Resources

Bücken, Hajo. 1995. *Button, button, who's got the button: 101 button games.* Edinburgh, Scotland: Floris Books.

Cole, Brock. 2000. *Buttons.* New York: Farrar, Straus and Giroux.

Freeman, Don. 1968. *Corduroy.* New York: The Viking Press.

Holtschlag, Margaret, and Carol Trojanowski. 1999. *Button crafts.* New York: Random House Pictureback Book.

Johnson, Traci Paige. 2000. *Blue's buttons.* Blue's Clues, vol. 6. New York: Simon and Schuster.

Lamstein, Sarah Marwil. 1999. *I like your buttons!* Morton Grove, Ill.: Albert Whitman.

Lobel, Arnold. 1970. *Frog and Toad are friends.* New York: HarperTrophy.

McNutt, Nan. 1997. *The button blanket: An activity book.* Seattle: Sasquatch Books.

Orgel, Doris. 1994. *Button soup.* New York: Bantam.

Reid, Margarette S. 1990. *The button box.* New York: Puffin Unicorn Books.

Sierra, Judy. 1999. *Tasty baby belly buttons.* New York: Dragonfly Books.

Taback, Simms. 1999. *Joseph had a little overcoat.* New York: Viking.

Williams, Rozanne Lanczak. 1994. *Buttons buttons.* Cypress, Calif.: Creative Teaching Press.

Babies

Cuddly, soft, bundled up tight,
Babies wake up all through the night.

Chubby cheeks, tufts of hair,
Babies carried everywhere.

Wiggling arms, fingers, and toes,
A baby has a button nose.

Crying, sighing, a soft coo:
Baby's sounds are just for you.

Let's pretend, and be babies for a while,
Get fed milk to make us smile;

Or practice being a mom or dad,
Hold baby close when she's feeling sad.

Bring on the babies, let's have fun
And play pat-a-cake 'til the day is done!

Theme Tree

Equipment for babies
cribs
high chairs
cradles
buggy, stroller
baskets—carried on back
slings

Baby names

Caring for baby
feeding—bottled formula,
    breast milk, pureed foods
clothes
bathing
play—mobiles, rattles,
    "pat-a-cake"

Baby safety
baby on back to sleep
support baby's head
baby gates, locks, outlet covers

Baby sounds
cries
burps
coo
baby rattles
musical toys

Weights and measures
weight
height
head circumference

Bedtime
lullabies

Mother Goose rhymes

Baby animals

Motion
moving
rocking
crawling
rolling over
bouncing

Introduction

You were once a baby, so was I and every child you will ever teach—so why not enjoy a unit on this universal experience? Babies have a lot to teach us, so open your eyes, your lap, and your hearts, and bring them on! Through ethnopediatrics, the study of parents, children, and childrearing across cultures, we learn that different cultures raise babies in different ways. According to Meredith Small (1999), professor of anthropology at Cornell University, there is no right or wrong style; behavior is either appropriate or inappropriate depending on that culture. While all babies have basically the same biological needs (sleep, food, emotional attachment), Small finds that these needs are being fulfilled in often dramatically different ways from culture to culture. So let's look at how babies are fed, carried, clothed, and stimulated around the globe, and enjoy the journey.

There are wonderful books, beautiful lullabies, and fun dramatic play props for this theme kit. I found it challenging to find accessible and affordable authentic materials representing other cultures and experiences when I built my own babies theme kit. The richness of this unit will depend on the resources available from the families you serve and the surrounding community. This is a wonderful opportunity to include babies with special needs. Appendix 2 includes People of Every Stripe, a company that makes dolls with adaptive equipment, including a doll who is fed through a g-tube. (A gastronomy tube—g-tube—is used to vent air from a child's stomach, or to deliver nutrition directly to the stomach.)

How will the children respond to this topic? Some will sneak the baby bottles and pacifiers into their own mouths when no one's looking. Some will love playing the parenting role: the nurturing, the fussing, the hovering. Others might take the opportunity to work on some sibling rivalry issues. You might enjoy a few weeks of quiet voices, as you can always remind them, "Shh! The babies are sleeping."

Kit Contents

A selection of books about babies

Talk, Baby! **(Ziefert)**—A book that takes a realistic look at the linguistic and physical developmental milestones of a new baby as her brother patiently guides us through the first fourteen months of her life.

Birth: World Celebrations and Ceremonies **(Spirn)**—Useful as a teacher resource, this book describes cultural traditions and ceremonies surrounding birth in ten countries.

***Just Like a Baby* (Bond)**—You'll be tempted to climb into the homemade cradle along with the rest of this extended family.

***Babies on the Move* (Canizares)**—A short picture book that has simple captions and captivating photos.

***Babies* (Canizares)**—Simple photos and captions describe babies' universal needs.

***Baby Science: How Babies Really Work!* (Douglas)**—The author demystifies babyhood using preschool language.

***My Baby* (Winter)**—"Listen, my baby, to the coo, coo, coo of the turtle-dove." Treat yourself to this lyrical text and boldly colored and textured description of preparing a *bogolan* cloth to wrap the new baby. Painting cloth with mud is a traditional craft of the Nakunte Diarra women of Mali.

***Brown Sugar Babies* (Smith)**—Full-page photographs show the beautiful spectrum of hues of black children. The author says, "It is my hope that by seeing the diversity of the black children, we will realize how many wonderful colors are represented, celebrate our diversity, and enjoy the sweetness and love that children add to life."

***A Ride on Mother's Back: A Day of Baby Carrying around the World* (Bernhard)**—On hips, shoulders, backs, chests, even heads, babies get carried to and fro. Ride along with babies from North America to Asia and all lands in between.

***The Babies Are Coming!* (Hest)**—Follow these babies through their antics as they prepare for a special trip.

***On the Day You Were Born* (Frasier)**—Each baby's arrival on earth is momentous, yet dwarfed by the grand scheme of the spinning earth.

***Welcoming Babies* (Knight)**—We sing, we kiss, we touch, we name—babies around the world are welcomed.

***Alphababies* (Golding)**—Meet twenty-six babies each introducing a letter of the alphabet.

***Hi, New Baby!* (Harris)**—These illustrations are so realistic that the characters and their emotions jump out of the book. For example, as the mom sits at the kitchen table with the whole family engaged in eating, we see the baby breastfeeding.

***Hush, Little Baby* (Halpern)**—Collage-like illustrations accompany the text of this traditional lullaby.

***Baby Talk* (Hiatt)**—Soft portrayals of a baby's daily life and touching encounters with his big brother illustrate this book.

***Eyes, Nose, Fingers, and Toes: A First Book All about You* (Hindley)**—A book with a delightful look at baby and toddler body parts and their uses.

Play props

baby bottles

baby cups, bowls, and utensils

baby clothes (include multicultural fabrics)

baby blankets

tub for bathing

fabric representing South America, Africa, and Asia, to make baby slings

baby toys—rattles (a large assortment for sorting), baby books, music makers

photos of women breastfeeding babies (for display)

Commercial products

Chinasprout Hug and Hold Baby puppet (a lifelike baby puppet in a quilted bunting—see appendix 2)

multicultural, realistic baby dolls

baby food grinder

dolls of different ethnicities with special needs including prosthesis, g-tubes, and colostomy bags

selection of lullabies from various countries

Signs to post

Peek-a-Boo

Girl

Boy

Mama

Dada

Baby

Other materials

baby slings

baby equipment (cradle, high chair, stroller, car seat)

baskets made for babies in various cultures

Facts about Babies

- Research has shown a vast difference in physical contact between parent and baby in different cultures. Babies are touched 20–25 percent of the day in traditional American parenting; 90 percent of the day in Korea; 93 percent of the day and 100 percent of the night for babies raised by the Ache Indians in the Mbaracayu Forest of northern Paraguay.
- In Mato Grosso, Brazil, the home of the Bororo people, parents and their baby do not eat for a few days after birth in hopes that this will help the baby cope with hunger.
- Some people in England believe that the day of the week of a baby's birth will influence his or her behavior. Hence the poem (one of many versions):

> *Monday's child is fair of face,*
> *Tuesday's child is full of grace,*
> *Wednesday's child is full of woe,*
> *Thursday's child has far to go,*
> *Friday's child is loving and giving,*
> *Saturday's child works hard for a living.*
> *The child that is born on the Sabbath day*
> *is bonnie, and blithe, and good, and gay.*

- Japanese parents give their children names to bring them good luck. Babies receive toy dogs as gifts to symbolize protection for the baby.
- In southwestern Nigeria, Yoruba babies are held by their feet and shaken three times to make them brave and strong. Newborn girls are kept in their homes for six days after birth, boys for eight days because the Yoruba people believe girls are stronger than boys.
- The Hopi Indians of North America use volcanic ash to make babies' skin clean and soft.
- In many cultures a tree is planted in honor of a birth. In Switzerland, an apple tree is often planted for a boy and a nut tree for a girl.
- In China, a baby is considered one year old at birth. A Chinese child's second birthday is an important event. Babies tell their own fortunes by picking from an assortment of objects placed around them.

Sources: Knight, Margy Burns, *Welcoming Babies* (Gardiner, Maine: Tilbury House, 1994); Siegen-Smith, Nikki, *Welcome to the World* (New York: Orchard Books, 1996); www.birthdaytraditions.com; www.indigenousbabies.com

Family Involvement

One way to include families in your program is to write letters. I think it is respectful to children if we include them in the process. At the very least, be sure children know exactly what the letter that is being sent home says, and choose a greeting that includes all the people living in a child's home (mom, dad, grandma, big sister, and so on). Other children might choose to fill in Dear _____ and sign their own names.

Dear _____,

We are working on a theme about babies. We want to learn about babies from all over the world. When you come into my room (child care), would you add your ideas to the Theme Tree?

Do you have any of these materials to loan or give to our class (child care) to help us enjoy this theme?

- fabric from other countries
- baby toys
- information on your family traditions
- baby accessories such as receiving blankets, a food grinder, baby clothes
- equipment such as a high chair, a car seat, baby gates
- baby carrier (backpack, sling, basket)

Here are some activities we will be doing:

- caring for baby dolls—bathing, feeding, playing
- pureeing baby food
- observing a real baby (any volunteers?)
- learning lullabies and nursery rhymes

Get ready to ask me these questions at the end of this unit of study:

- What do all babies need?
- How are babies carried in some other countries?
- What is a baby telling you by crying?
- What is your favorite lullaby?

Thanks for all your help.

Your daughter (son),

P.S. Don't be surprised if I start using baby talk and acting like a baby for a few weeks—I'm just playacting!

Ready, Set, Go!

Daily routines

Arrival

Collect baby photos from the children. Make copies (so you don't damage original photos) and prepare Welcome Baby cards. When children arrive, they can post their cards on the baby board.

Breakfast

Children can take turns feeding each other with close supervision.

Circle

Try good old-fashioned "pat-a-cake" clapping games.

Free choice

See the interest areas described below.

Small group time

Explore baby toys. Talk about shapes, colors, action words (push, pull, poke), and more.

Rest time

Play or sing some soothing lullabies.

Interest areas

Dramatic play

- baby equipment
- baby dishes, utensils
- empty boxes of baby food (an assortment of ethnic foods)
- baby clothes, dolls, blankets

Manipulative and math center

- Provide nesting cups.
- Fill baby bottles with different amounts of water and place in order from least to most full.
- Fold old-fashioned baby diapers (fold in half, and half again).
- Count and sort baby socks.

Art and projects

- Babies can see black and white for the first few months. They are attracted to strong, bold patterns. Put black and white paint at the easels.

Sensory station

- Invite a baby, and children will use their senses to observe. They can get an idea of the sweetness of breast milk by adding a teaspoon of sugar to a cup or so of warm milk.
- Let children apply baby powder and baby lotion.
- Make baby cereal and ask children to describe its taste and texture.
- Water temperature is important at bathtime, and milk temperature is important at feeding time. Teach children how to test water and milk for warm temperature. Introduce a water thermometer.

Library

- See the list of books in Kit Contents.

New discoveries

- How absorbent are diapers? Try an experiment with different brands of diapers. How much water can they absorb before they become saturated? Share your results with parents.

Writing center

- Set out a large picture collection of babies doing different activities and showing different emotions. Provide blank books made of construction paper. Children can use the pictures to make their own books about babies.

Music and movement

- What kind of music do babies like? Ask parents to send in some of their favorite music.
- Have an assortment of musical baby toys available.
- Introduce multicultural lullabies.

Activity Ideas

Baby food

Babies need to eat soft foods. Making baby food is simple, and the results are nutritious and economical. Try recipes from the Wholesome Baby Foods Web site for starters (see Resources).

Rattle sorting

Collect baby rattles. Be sure to have an assortment of rattles in different materials (plastic, wood, cloth, and maybe even silver), colors, and sounds. Explore ways to sort the rattles, discussing names for color and other attributes. Teach children how to make tally marks; chart sorting results (material, color, sound, and so on).

What's in a rattle?

Collect plastic soda bottles or wide-mouth juice bottles. Wash and dry them thoroughly. Let children experiment with filling the bottles with different items. Provide aquarium stones, rice, sand, beans, and other small objects. Children can use scoops and funnels to fill bottles. Lids can be glued on. What conclusions can the children draw? Does a full bottle make as much sound as a less-full bottle? What material or quantity makes the loudest sound? Which bottle was hardest to fill?

Resources

Bernhard, Emery, and Durga Bernhard. 1996. *A ride on mother's back: A day of baby carrying around the world.* San Diego: Harcourt Brace and Co.

Bond, Rebecca. 1999. *Just like a baby.* Boston: Little, Brown and Co.

Canizares, Susan. 1999. *Babies.* New York: Scholastic.

————. 1999. *Babies on the move.* New York: Scholastic.

Douglas, Ann. 1998. *Baby science: How babies really work!* New York: Firefly Books.

Feldman, Eve B. 1996. *Birthdays! Celebrating life around the world.* Mahwah, N.J.: BridgeWater Books.

Frasier, Debra. 1991. *On the day you were born.* San Diego: Harcourt Brace Jovanovich.

Golding, Kim. 1998. *Alphababies.* New York: Dorling Kindersley.

Halpern, Shari. 1997. *Hush, little baby.* New York: North-South Books.

Harris, Robie. 2000. *Hi, new baby!* Cambridge, Mass.: Candlewick Press.

Hest, Amy. 1997. *The babies are coming.* New York: Crown.

Hiatt, Fred. 1999. *Baby talk.* New York: Margaret K. McElderry Books.

Hindley, Judy. 1999. *Eyes, nose, fingers, and toes: A first book all about you.* Cambridge, Mass.: Candlewick Press.

Knight, Margy Burns. 1994. *Welcoming babies.* Gardiner, Maine: Tilbury House Publishers.

Look, Lenore. 2001. *Henry's first-moon birthday.* New York: Simon and Schuster Children's Books.

Myers, Susan. 2001. *Everywhere babies.* San Diego: Harcourt Brace.

Osofsky, Audrey. 1992. *Dreamcatcher.* New York: Orchard Books.

Siegen-Smith, Nikki. 1996. *Welcome to the world: A celebration of birth and babies from many cultures.* New York: Orchard Books.

Small, Meredith. 1999. *Our babies, ourselves: How biology and culture shape the way we parent.* New York: Doubleday and Co.

Smith, Charles. 2000. *Brown sugar babies.* New York: Jump at the Sun.

Spirn, Michele. 1999. *Birth: World celebrations and ceremonies.* Woodbridge, Conn.: Blackbirch Press.

Winter, Jeanette. 2001. *My baby.* New York: Farrar, Straus and Giroux.

Ziefert, Harriet. 1999. *Talk, baby!* New York: Henry Holt and Company.

Recordings

Chinese lullabies. 1996. Taiwan: Wind Records.

Cuban lullaby. 2000. New York: Ellipsis Arts.

Lullabies of Latin America. 1999. Los Angeles: Rhino Records.

Under the green corn moon: Native American lullabies. 1998. Boulder, Colo.: Silver Wave. Many different tribes represented.

Naptime

I think naps should be for grownups, not me:
They are always yawning and being grouchy!

Maybe they need a rest, time to close their eyes;
The owl sleeps in the day, and he's so wise.

Why do parents and teachers think I need a nap,
Just because I like to cuddle and climb in their lap?

When I'm tired, you'll be the first to know;
I'm not sleepy just 'cause you say so!

I'm busy playing, learning, and exercising my brain;
I have to read more books, and finish building my train.

I don't have time to rest and lie on a cot:
Can't you see I have to accomplish a lot?

What, you say there will be a snack when I awake?
I'll still have time to play with Jasmine and Blake?

My teachers and friends will all still be here?
Well, why didn't you tell me I have nothing to fear?

My eyes are feeling droopy, my legs are like Jell-o.
Can you get me my blanky, Pooh bear, and pillow?

I might just close my eyes and rest, if that's okay with you,
But don't worry, I'll be up soon, because there's so much to do!

Theme Tree

Songs
Hush Little Baby
Hush-a-Bye Baby

Classic stories and nursery rhymes
Sleeping Beauty
Wee Willie Winkie
Diddle Diddle Dumpling, My Son John
The Princess and the Pea
Bye-bye, Baby Bunting
Twinkle, Twinkle, Little Star

Nighttime fears
dark
monsters
shadows
being alone

Light up the night
flashlights
fireflies
light sticks
nightlights
glow-in-the-dark stars
black light

Nighttime clothes
pajamas
nightgown
bedroom slippers
robe

Quiet/Loud
instruments
kitchen devices
country sounds/city
  sounds

Cultural sleep traditions

Places to sleep
train—sleeping car
ship—bunk
tent—sleeping bag
spaceship
forest
barn
water

Sleeping props
futon
blanket
quilt
pillow
hammock
cradle
crib
mattress

Introduction

Naptime can be the best or worst time of your day. I've been in enough child care settings to know it is surely not the easiest time! You are tired, they are tired. It sounds simple. Say, "It's naptime," and children should happily go off to their cots or mats, settle down, and fall into a restful sleep. If this is not an accurate depiction of your children, you are not alone.

The naptime theme kit is filled with tips, props, and stories to bring the best out of you and your children at this time of day. The kit also extends the focus into the general topic of sleep. This allows you to explore animals and their sleep habits, nighttime, darkness, and all that goes along with naps.

So, dim the lights, kick up your feet, and start to visualize an idyllic naptime. Zzzzzzzzz.

Kit Contents

A selection of sleep-related stories

Time for Bed **(Fox)**—All the earth's children are lulled to sleep.

Bedtime for Frances **(Hoban)**—Treat yourself and the children to the audiocassette version of this story—one of my all-time favorites.

Asleep, Asleep **(Ginsburg)**—Dreamy pictures and sparse words make this the perfect sleep book.

A South African Night **(Isadora)**—The animals in South Africa come to life as a bustling day in Johannesburg comes to a halt.

The Napping House **(Wood)**—Let the author and illustrator take you on this fun, dreamlike napping adventure.

The Little Quiet Book **(Ross)**—This is a tiny book full of quiet images.

There's a Nightmare in my Closet **(Mayer)**—This is one of my favorite Mercer Mayer books, featuring monsters that you wouldn't mind meeting at night. Prepare what you will say about the little boy's toy cannon and pop gun, if needed.

Where the Wild Things Are **(Sendak)**

Goodnight Moon **(Brown)**

***The Quilt Story* (Johnston)**—Experience the long-lasting comfort a quilt can provide.

***The Big Yawn* (Faulkner)**—Follow animals from small to big to bigger as they take that last wide-mouthed yawn before bed.

***Can't You Sleep Little Bear?* (Waddell)**—This little bear's nighttime fear gets resolved with a little help from mom and the moon.

***Who Sleeps in the City?* (Bertrand)**—Peek at city-dwelling animals bedded down for the night.

***Sleepy Bears* (Fox)**—Each of the cubs get their very own poem to lull them to sleep; be careful, you might end up hibernating yourself.

***The Legend of Sleeping Bear* (Wargin)**—A bestselling rendition of an Ojibwe Indian tale, the story takes place on Lake Michigan.

***Peeping and Sleeping* (Manushkin)**—Sometimes bedtime warrants a little outdoor exploration; follow Barry and his dad on their moonlit walk.

***The Berenstain Bears: In The Dark* (Berenstain)**—This animated video tells the story of Papa Bear helping Sister conquer her fears of sleeping in the dark.

Teacher resources

***Think of Something Quiet* (Cherry)**—Bring serenity into your classroom or home with this guide.

***Bear Hugs for Nap Time* (Claycomb)**—This Totline gem is filled with creative activities to bring out the best of you and the children at naptime.

***Practical Solutions to Practically Every Problem: The Early Childhood Teacher's Manual* (Saifer)**—See chapter 10, "Peaceful Nap Times."

***Caring Spaces, Learning Places: Children's Environments That Work* (Greenman)**—See the section on Sleeping.

***The Creative Curriculum for Infants and Toddlers* (Dombro, Colker, and Dodge)**—Chapter 14, "Sleeping and Naptime," covers such topics as handling crying at naptime, responding to a child who doesn't sleep, and communicating effectively with families about sleep issues.

Lullabies and sleepy music

See Resources list on page 132 for more multicultural lullabies.

African Lullaby

Dreamship, K. L. Gifford

Quiet Places, Hap Palmer

Dreamosaurus

Baby's Bedtime

Aladdin, **Walt Disney**—The song "On a Dark Night" is nice for movement with bracelet streamers (see Activity Ideas).

Play props

nightgowns

pajamas

slippers

robes

sleeping mats or sleeping bags

eye mask

stuffed bears

bedtime books

cradle

blankets

string of lights

Signs to post

SHHH! BABY SLEEPING

SHHH! BEARS HIBERNATING

Other materials

mosquito net (used for sleeping in some climates)

futon

Tips about Nap or Rest Time

- Consider using the word *rest* instead of *nap,* which has a negative connotation to some children.

- Schedule rest time early enough so that the children are not overly tired.

- Use a soft, tingly bell to signal "time to tiptoe to your cot or mat."

- Try settling the atmosphere with small twinkle lights that only go on when it is quiet.

- Allow soft quiet toys on the mats to help children settle down.

- For children who don't fall asleep, offer them "quiet bags" filled with small toys for imaginative play. Use soft-sided lunch bags (available in dollar or discount stores) and a collection of small books and toys.

- An eye mask might help children who have a hard time tuning out visual stimulation. For sanitary reasons, these should not be shared. Ask for parent volunteers to sew them using scraps of soft material and elastic across the backs of the masks.

- Tell the children what to expect or look forward to when rest time is over.

- Share rest-time successes with parents—they may be able to use some of the ideas at home.

Family Involvement

One way to include families in your program is to write letters. I think it is respectful to children if we include them in the process. At the very least, be sure children know exactly what the letter that is being sent home says, and choose a greeting that includes all the people living in a child's home (mom, dad, grandma, big sister, and so on). Other children might choose to fill in Dear _____ and sign their own names.

Dear _____,

We are learning all about sleep and napping in my class. If those are two topics you are interested in, please come into my room (child care) and add your ideas to the Napping Theme Tree.

Do you have any of these materials to loan or give to our class (child care) to help us enjoy this theme?

- eye masks (we need a volunteer parent to sew one for each child)
- baby blanket
- holiday or other strings of lights
- favorite bedtime stories
- soothing music, such as classical music or nature sounds

Here are some activities we will be doing:

- counting sheep and other favorite animals
- talking about our nighttime fears
- learning about sleep habits of animals

Get ready to ask me these questions at the end of this unit of study:

- What animal sleeps upside down? What animals sleep during the day?
- Why do some people sleep under mosquito nets?
- Why is sleep important for me?

Thanks for all your help.

Your daughter (son),

Ready, Set, Go!

Daily routines

Arrival

Invite children to wear their pajamas to school one day.

Circle

Introduce the "Naptime" poem. Invite children to show off the pajamas they are wearing and talk about their bedtime routines at home.

Free play

See the interest areas described below.

Small group time

Experiment with quiet and loud sounds. As much as we tell children to be quiet, we don't spend any time teaching the concept. Present a box of items that make sounds and sort them into quiet and loud groups. There will be some items that you can make sound quiet or loud. Try a whistle, rainstick, air coming out of a balloon, stethoscope to listen to heartbeat, cell-phone ringer turned on loud or soft, cymbals, and so on.

Lunch

Focus on the sounds of eating: crunching, slurping, sipping, and chewing.

Rest time

Play a tape of nature's sounds. There are also wonderful selections of lullabies from many cultures available through libraries, children's music catalogs, and Web sites.

Interest areas

Dramatic play

- See play props listed in Kit Contents.

Manipulative and math center

- Provide a flannelboard with ten cutout bears and a big bed. Teach the song "There Were Ten in the Bed":

There were ten in the bed and the little one said,
"Roll over, roll over."
So they all rolled over and one fell out.
There were nine in the bed and the little one said,
"Roll over, roll over."
So they all rolled over and one fell out.

(Continue until the last verse, which goes as follows.)

There was one in the bed, and he said,
"Goodnight, sleep tight."

Art and projects

- Provide dark colors and star stickers at the easel so that children can make "night sky" pictures. Turn the lights down low during play time. Notice how dim light affects the mood of the day?

Sensory station

- Have children's eye masks (see Kit Contents) available in this area. Suggest that the children try playing with modeling clay, or fingerpainting with paint or shaving cream with their eyes covered. Help them focus on the relaxed feeling, the quiet, and the sensations.

Library

- See the list of books in Kit Contents.
- Add teddy bears and blankets to the library area.

New discoveries

- Bring in some dirt and earthworms. Make a worm bin (instructions can be found online or in books or gardening magazines). Talk about the work that worms do quietly in the dark.

Writing center

- Provide books that illustrate nighttime fears and dreams, such as *Where the Wild Things Are* and *There's a Nightmare in My Closet*. Children can dictate or write stories about their dream experiences. Have a word list available including *sleep, monster, dark, scared, dream,* and more as children request them.

Music and movement

- Provide scarves (chiffon-like material works best), bracelet streamers (see Activity Ideas), feathers, and other quiet props for movement to soft music.

Activity Ideas

Quiet quilt

Begin this project by showing children some samples of quilts. Ask families to bring quilts from home. Ask the children to help you make a patchwork quilt by piecing together squares of material. Children will have an opportunity to decorate their own squares with things that make them think of quiet. Brainstorm a list of quiet images, such as the moon, stars, a feather, caterpillars, a sleeping baby, and snowflakes.

This can be a take-home or an in-school project. Think creatively about materials children can use to decorate their fabric squares. Teachers can use a glue gun to secure items to the fabric, or children can use craft glue.

The Quiet Quilt can come out at naptime and be hung from a clothesline to help children quiet down.

Bracelet streamers

Children can make their own bracelet streamers and keep them in the music and movement area. Waving the streamers makes a peaceful and relaxing activity before or after nap.

Use plastic lids about the size of an eight-ounce yogurt container's. Cut out the middle of each lid, leaving just the outer rim. You can also use children's plastic bangle bracelets (they come in sets of ten or twelve and are available at discount stores).

Give each child a "bracelet" to decorate with streamers. Children can choose colored ribbons, crepe paper streamers, or paper streamers to tape to their bracelets. They can cut or tear any length they want, as long as the streamers are not longer than their height (so that they don't trip).

Hold the bracelets in your hands and wave the streamers.

Shadows

Introduce the concept of shadows by going outside on a sunny day and having the children discover them. Some cultural references to shadows are the story of Peter Pan, Groundhog Day, and the poem "My Shadow," by Robert Louis Stevenson.

Find a spot outside or where the sun shines into your classroom.

Measure each child's shadow as the child stands in the same spot early in the morning, at lunchtime, and at the end of the day.

Make a chart or drawing showing the different shapes and directions of the shadow at different times of the day.

Shine a bright light on a white wall, large paper, or bed sheet (an overhead projector works well). Let children experiment with hand and puppet shadows.

Resources

The Berenstain bears: In the dark. 1989. Video. New York: Random House.

Bertrand, Lynne. 1997. *Who sleeps in the city?* Boston: Houghton Mifflin.

Brown, Margaret Wise. 1991. *Goodnight moon.* New York: HarperCollins.

Cherry, Clare. 1981. *Think of something quiet.* Carthage, Ill.: Fearon Teachers Aids.

Claycomb, Patty. 1994. *Bear hugs for nap time.* Everett, Wash.: Warren Publishing House.

Dombro, Amy Laura, Laura J. Colker, and Diane Trister Dodge. 1997. *The creative curriculum for infants and toddlers.* Washington, D.C.: Teaching Strategies.

Faulkner, Keith, and Jonathan Lambert. 1999. *The big yawn.* Brookfield, Conn.: Millbrook Press.

Fox, Mem. 1997. *Time for bed.* San Diego: Red Wagon Books/Harcourt Brace.

———. 1999. *Sleepy bears.* San Diego: Harcourt Brace.

Ginsburg, Mirra. 1992. *Asleep, asleep.* New York: Greenwillow Books.

Greenman, Jim. 1988. *Caring spaces, learning places: Children's environments that work.* Redmond, Wash.: Child Care Information Exchange.

Hoban, Russell. 1995. *Bedtime for Frances.* New York: HarperCollins Children's Books.

Isadora, Rachel. 1998. *A South African night.* New York: Greenwillow Books.

Johnston, Tony. 1985. *The quilt story.* New York: Penguin Putnam Books for Young Readers.

Manushkin, Fran. 1994. *Peeping and sleeping.* New York: Clarion Books.

Mayer, Mercer. 1968. *There's a nightmare in my closet.* New York: Dial Books for Young Readers.

Ross, Katherine. 1989. *The little quiet book.* New York: Random House, Inc.

Saifer, Steffen. 1991. *Practical solutions to practically every problem: The early childhood teacher's manual.* St. Paul: Redleaf Press.

Sendak, Maurice. 1963. *Where the wild things are.* New York: HarperCollins Publishers.

Waddell, Martin. 1994. *Can't you sleep, little bear?* Cambridge, Mass.: Candlewick Press.

Wargin, Kathy-Jo. 1998. *The legend of Sleeping Bear.* Chelsea, Mich.: Sleeping Bear Press.

Wood, Audrey. 1984. *The napping house.* San Diego: Harcourt Brace.

Recordings

African lullaby. 1999. New York: Ellipsis Arts.

Aladdin. 1992. Burbank, Calif.: Disney Records.

Collins, Judy. 1990. *Baby's bedtime.* New York: Lightyear Records.

Dreamosaurus. 1998. Cambridge, Mass.: Rounder Records.

Gifford, Kathie Lee. 1995. *Dreamship.* New York: Time Warner Kids.

Palmer, Hap. 1992. *Quiet places.* Topanga, Calif.: Hap-Pal Music, Inc.

Theme Kit 9

Family

Who's in your family, who lives with you?
Do you have an Aunt Mary, Sasha, or Sue?

Who lives with you in the place you call home?
Who takes care of you so you're not alone?

Do you have a family of two, three, or more?
Say their names so we know for sure.

A mom, dad, and sister makes three,
But wait a minute, don't forget me!

Count the people in your family carefully,
And then make a beautiful family tree.

Theme Tree

Activities/Hobbies
music
collecting
sports
reading
storytelling

Languages

Family celebrations

Families around the world
houses
types of food
transportation
children/schools

People
mother
father
grandparents
aunts/uncles
cousins
stepsister/brother/mother/
  father

Jobs/Chores
laundry
cooking
grocery shopping
cleaning
gardening

Family pets

Introduction

This is probably the most familiar concept to children, yet the most confusing. What defines one family doesn't apply to all or even most. Here are some definitions; see how they hold up to your ideas.

Family: A fundamental social group in society typically consisting of parents and their offspring. 2. All the members of a household under one roof (American Heritage College Dictionary 1993).

A family is a group of two or more people joined by bonds of love and/or kinship (Kostelnik 1991).

My preference is the last: the simplest, most inclusive definition.

This kit doesn't include a fact sheet, because the "facts" about families are different in every group of children! For family facts, you can take either of two approaches. The first is to gather facts from the families that are currently in your program. These facts could take the form of family photos, with the caption, "Our family includes . . . ." You could ask each family to fill out some brief information about their family life, such as what holidays they celebrate, or what their favorite dinner is, or where they like to go on the weekends.

The second option is to explore facts about family life here and around the world. You can narrow the focus to food, play, homes, or work, and then investigate similarities and differences in how families do the things that all people have in common. The danger with this approach is that you have to be very attentive that the unit doesn't turn into "tourist curriculum" that encourages children to learn "exotic" facts about people in other parts of the world (which may or may not be true of all people in a given area). This approach is most appropriate if you have families from many different cultures in your program, which gives you the opportunity to learn about various cultures in the context of real people the children know and can talk to.

This kit fits in the "traditional" category. Families are talked about in every preschool class; the topic spans the tests of time, culture, and inclusion. No one is left out of this topic. Families come in many colors and sizes. They work and play. They eat and sleep. They live in different types of shelters, speak different languages, and eat different foods. Celebrate the differences; marvel at the sameness.

If you like people watching and travel, you'll like this theme. It's full of interesting people, places, and things.

Kit Contents

A selection of books about families

A Family for Jamie: An Adoption Story **(Bloom)**

I Love You Like Crazy Cakes **(Lewis)**—This book features an international adoption story.

No Mirrors in My Nana's House **(Barnwell)**—"I only knew love and I never knew hate" was the lesson learned at Nana's house.

Kevin and His Dad **(Smalls)**—This book explores a day in the life of a dad and his son.

Black Is Brown Is Tan **(Adoff)**—"This is the way it is for us, this is the way we are;" a poetic view of an interracial family.

Amber's Other Grandparents **(Bonnici)**—Amber's grandparents come from India to visit Amber, who lives in America.

How My Family Lives in America **(Kuklin)**—Sanu, Eric, and April all live and play in America. They celebrate their family traditions and share their new American traditions.

Best Best Colors **(Hoffman)**—Nate's two moms help him learn that he can have more than one favorite color, and more than one best friend.

Mama Zooms **(Cowen-Fletcher)**—Some mommies walk and some mommies zoom. Take a ride with this mom in her wheelchair.

That's a Family—You might need to hold a fund-raiser to buy this 35-minute film documentary, but it will be worth it. This candid look at fifty beautiful family variations is geared for the K–6 population, and would work well for staff and parent sensitivity training.

Related books

Houses and Homes **(Morris)**—A photo essay featuring a variety of houses from around the world.

Loving **(Morris)**—Another photo essay by Ann Morris, which features people from many cultures showing love for each other.

Everybody Cooks Rice **(Dooley)**

Everybody Bakes Bread **(Dooley)**

Play props

telephones

pretend cameras

small mailbox

pots

wok

tortilla warmer

broom, mop, bucket, other household tools

workbench tools

garden tools

jump ropes

mancala (an ancient counting game with many cultural variations)

spinning tops (collect a variety from different countries, of different materials)

Commercial products

See appendix 2 for information on how to find products.

Block Play People sets (Lakeshore Learning Materials; *see* dramatic play activities)

family puppet sets

flannelboard family pieces

poster sets

Other materials

multicultural music and instruments

articles of clothing

cooking utensils

special tools that you collect from families

Family Involvement

One way to include families in your program is to write letters. I think it is respectful to children if we include them in the process. At the very least, be sure children know exactly what the letter that is being sent home says, and choose a greeting that includes all the people living in a child's home (mom, dad, grandma, big sister, and so on). Other children might choose to fill in Dear _____ and sign their own names.

Dear _____,

We are working on a theme about families. We want to learn all about our family and my friends' families. When you come into my room (child care), would you add your ideas to the Theme Tree?

Do you have any of the following materials to loan or give to our class (child care) to help us enjoy this theme?

- special tools for cooking or other activities
- our favorite family game

Here are some activities we will be doing:

- cooking family recipes
- looking at different family houses
- meeting family members
- tasting many types of bread

Get ready to ask me these questions at the end of this unit of study:

- What is special about our family? How are some families different?
- Do you know who my mother is? my sister/brother? (build understanding of family relationships)
- What special way do we say goodnight at our house?

Thanks for all your help.

Your daughter (son),

Ready, Set, Go!

Daily routines

Arrival

Encourage parents to send in different family members during this theme for pickup and drop-off time.

Circle

Introduce finger plays about family members. Adapt "Thumbkin" to use family names.

Free choice

See the interest areas described below.

Outdoor play

Give children rollers and wide paint brushes with water so they can pretend to paint the outside of the building, the way a house might be painted.

Small group time

Practice family chores: sort laundry, wash dishes, shop for food.

Lunch

Invite children to bring bread from home. Compare the varieties (even if it's just white, wheat, and rye).

Rest time

Invite a parent to tell a bedtime story.

Interest areas

Dramatic play

- Provide family block "people" (see Kit Contents): each family set of different ethnicities has eight family members. Supplement family sets with a set of eight block play people with different physical abilities; puzzle set includes eight puzzles depicting diverse family groupings (single-parent families, physical differences, extended families).

Manipulative and math center

- Provide family theme puzzles.

Art and projects

● Use pictures cut from magazines to make family collages.

Library

● See the list of books in Kit Contents.

New discoveries

● Make fingerprints. Use magnifying glasses to inspect and compare them.

Writing center

● Ask parents to send in informal or first names of extended family members (Aunt Bertha, Grandma, Granddad, Cousin Stanley). Invite children to dictate sentences about each family member.

Music and movement

● Pretend you are having a family wedding. Dance up a storm!

Activity Ideas

Family photo cubes

Purchase cube-shaped gift boxes from a party store. Children can stuff each box with tissue paper or newspaper to make it sturdy. On each surface of a box, children draw the face of a family member (photos can be used if available). Markers work better than crayons on a glossy box surface. If there are too many surfaces, the child decorates the extra space; if there are not enough spaces, the child uses a second box.

What's in a name?

This is a great opportunity to focus on last names. A little bit of history will add some fun to this activity. Where did our last names come from? Almost half of the American population has a name that relates to a location. The location was either the physical description of someone's surroundings or the description of the family's country of origin. An example would be William, who lived by a hill and became William Hill. If he lived near a forest, he might have been named William Woods. Many people who came from other countries carried an adaptation of their town name with them. Joseph from Naples could become Joseph Napoli (Wolfman 1991).

Collect pictures that show people in different physical settings. Children can make up a first name and then add a last name based on some physical feature in the background. How about Tom Iceberg, Nancy Mountain, or Lawrence Lake?

Family fruit salad

America used to be known as the "melting pot" because of all the different immigrant groups who settled here and adopted American lifestyles. A more recent term is the American "tossed salad." We are a country made up of many different types of people who all maintain their uniqueness and their individuality.

Make a fruit salad to honor the combined delights that each family brings to the classroom. Each family contributes something unique while making up the whole. Request that each family send in a fruit to be added to a fruit salad. Children can help wash and prepare the fruit and enjoy the feast.

Resources

Adoff, Arnold. 1973. *Black is brown is tan.* New York: HarperCollins Publishers.

American Heritage college dictionary, The. 3d ed. 1993. Boston: Houghton Mifflin.

Barnwell, Ysaye. 1998. *No mirrors in my nana's house.* San Diego: Harcourt Brace and Co.

Bloom, Suzanne. 1991. *A family for Jamie: An adoption story.* New York: Crown Publishers, Inc.

Bonnici, Peter. 1985. *Amber's other grandparents.* London: The Bodley Head Ltd.

Cowen-Fletcher, Jane. 1996. *Mama zooms.* New York: Scholastic Books.

Dooley, Norah. 1992. *Everybody cooks rice.* Minneapolis: Lerner Publishing Group.

———. 1996. *Everybody bakes bread.* Minneapolis: Lerner Publishing Group.

Hoffman, Eric. 1999. *Best best colors.* St. Paul: Redleaf Press.

Kostelnik, Marjorie, ed. 1997. *Teaching young children using themes.* Glenview, Ill.: Scott, Foresman and Co.

Kuklin, Susan. 1992. *How my family lives in America.* New York: Bradbury Press.

Lewis, Rose A. 2000. *I love you like crazy cakes.* New York: Little Brown and Co.

Morris, Ann. 1990. *Loving.* New York: Lothrop, Lee and Shepard Books.

———. 1992. *Houses and homes.* New York: Lothrop, Lee and Shepard Books.

Smalls, Irene. 1999. *Kevin and his dad.* New York: Scholastic.

That's a family. 2000. Video. San Francisco: Women's Educational Media.

Wolfman, Ira. 1991. *Do people grow on family trees? Genealogy for kids and other beginners.* New York: Workman Publishing Company.

Appendix 1

Blank Theme Tree

Theme Tree

Appendix 2

Catalogs, Products, and Web Sites

Not every catalog and product listed here is referenced in the book, but everything mentioned in the book can be found here. This list includes some of my personal favorites; it is by no means complete.

10 Acres Backyard Dairy Farm, www.10acresbackyard.com; family dairy farmers in Kentucky offer real-life experiences in farming.

American Printing House for the Blind, www.aph.org, Louisville, KY; sells a good abacus for use with young children.

Animal Town, www.animaltown.com, Greenland, NH, 800-445-8642; carefully selected play items fostering cooperative play and learning.

As on TV Products, www.asontv.com, 800-368-3763; The Original Buttoneer.

Asia for Kids, www.asiaforkids.com, Cincinnati, OH, 800-888-9681; best resources about Asia and the world for parents and educators.

Barefoot Books, www.barefoot-books.com, New York, NY, 212-604-0505; stunning books and posters representing and honoring diverse cultures.

Best Children's Music, www.bestchildrensmusic.com; high-quality children's music by age group and related sources; includes audio samples; see "Great Big Sun," "I've Got Imagination," "I Will Hold Your Tiny Hand," and "40 Winks."

Bilingual Books for Kids, www.bilingualbooks.com, 800-385-1020; selection of picture books with side-by-side Spanish and English text; titles include "Cenicienta/Cinderella," "Caperucita roja/Little Red Riding Hood," "Los tres cerdos/The Three Pigs."

Blackbirch Press, www.blackbirch.com, 303-387-7525; educational books with library binding; see *Sneakers, Letters Home from . . . ,* Bear series.

The Book Vine for Children, www.bookvine.com, McHenry, IL, 800-772-4220; carefully selected books for infants, toddlers, and preschoolers.

California Rice Commission, www.calrice.org; see section for educators.

Celebrate the Child, www.celebratechild.com, 800-237-8400; Guatemalan baby bib and booties, Russian baby rattle, and other items from around the world.

Charnstrom Mail Center Solutions, www.charnstrom.com, Shakopee, MN, 800-328-2962; unique storage options for kits, vinyl mailbags.

Child Wood, www.childwoodmagnets.com, Bainbridge Island, WA, 800-362-9825; magnetized storytelling sets.

ChinaSprout, www.chinasprout.com, Brooklyn, NY, 718-439-7278; Chinese cultural and educational products; Hug and Hold Baby puppet.

Confetti Company, P.O. Box 1155, Studio City, CA 91614, 818-783-6253; books and animated videos featuring multiethnic characters, nonviolent, bias-free stories.

Constructive Playthings, www.constplay.com, Grandview, MO, 800-448-7830; early childhood educational toys, equipment, art supplies, and teaching aids.

Crystal Productions, Glenview, IL, 800-255-8629; highest quality laminated art posters for teaching art and culture to children.

The English Teacher's Assistant, www.etanewsletter.com; a newsletter for ESL and EFL teachers and tutors.

Folkmanis, www.folkmanis.com, Emeryville, CA, 510-658-7677 (minimum order $200); high-quality puppets.

For Kidz Only, www.forkidzonly.com, Tacoma, WA, 800-979-8898; architecurally correct block sets—Japanese, Russian, Egyptian, and more.

Happy Baby Products, www.happybabyproducts.com, 800-549-8973; baby food grinder.

Harvest Book Company, www.harvestbooks.com, Fort Washington, PA, 800-563-1222; hard-to-find or out-of-print books.

The Hay Exchange, www.hayexchange.com; price and locate hay by state.

HearthSong, www.hearthsong.com, Grand Rapids, MI, 800-325-2502; interesting selection of playful items for children of all ages.

Heptune Lyrics, www.heptune.com/lyrics; contains lyrics to "Button Up Your Overcoat," among other songs.

The History of Cotton, www.cottonman.com; purchase a boll of cotton.

HobbyScience Amalgam's Science Projects for Kids, www.pages.ivillage.com/mindmeld; science projects for kids.

Indigenous Babies, www.indigenousbabies.com, Orlando, FL, 877-695-8369; Maya baby carrier.

Justbabies, www.justbabies.com, Seattle, WA, 888-900-2229; Khanga baby slings.

KIDiddles, www.kididdles.com; database of children's song lyrics and music resources.

Kids Farms, www.kidsfarm.com; children can learn about farms and animals at this site, which is based on a working farm in Colorado.

Learning Curve, www.learningcurve.com, 312-981-7000; a nonprofit organization dedicated to creative play; features FELTKids, Small Miracles (high-end dress-up clothes), and Kid Classics (quality wooden puzzles and cooperative games; replacement pieces readily available).

Learning Materials Workshop, www.learningmaterialswork.com, Burlington, VT, 800-693-7164; materials crafted from maple and birch hardwoods, encourages high-level thinking and building.

Lehman's, www.lehmans.com, Kidron, OH, 888-780-4975; Lehman's "Good Neighbor Heritage" Non-electric Catalog.

Magic Cabin Dolls, www.magiccabin.com, Grand Rapids, MI, 888-623-6557; handmade, high-quality, one-of-a-kind play items.

National Association for the Education of Young Children Early Childhood Resources Catalog, www.naeyc.org, Washington, DC, 800-424-2460.

North Canton City Schools Farm Unit, www.viking.stark.k12.oh.us; click on Orchard Hill Elementary to view their farm theme unit.

People of Every Stripe, Portland, OR, 800-282-0612; dolls with a range of disabilities and ethnicities.

Putumayo World Music, www.worldplayground.com; high-quality, authentic multicultural music for children.

The Puzzle People, www.puzzlepeopleinc.com, 706-374-3358; quality wooden puzzles and game sets and replacement pieces.

Puzzles Plus, Inc., www.puzzlesplus.net, Beavercreek, OH, 800-770-8283; wooden puzzles with knobs, pegs, magnetic pieces; window puzzles.

Rhythm Band Instruments, www.rhythmband.com, Fort Worth, TX, 800-424-4724.

Rigby, www.rigby.com, Crystal Lake, IL, 800-822-8661; early literacy books, very good selection of unbiased fairy tales (see selection of Pebble Soup books).

Roots and Wings, www.rootsandwingscatalog.com, Boulder, CO, 800-833-1787; books and products that celebrate diversity; three-in-one storytelling dolls.

Scholastic Supplementary Materials, www.scholastic.com, Jefferson City, MO, 800-724-6527; wide variety of picture books.

Small World Toys, Culver City, CA, 800-421-4153; Cinderella Puzzle; offers replacement pieces.

The Story Teller Felt Educational Products, www.funfelt.com, 877-643-5521; classic stories and rhymes, audiotapes, felt sets, felt masks. Includes mask sets for Three Little Pigs, Little Red Riding Hood, and Goldilocks.

Storytime Dolls, www.storytimedolls.com; three-way storytelling dolls, puppet sets.

The Straight Edge, Inc., www.straightedgeinc.com, Brooklyn, NY, 800-643-2794; features "Inside, Outside" puzzles and Read a Mat place mats; minimum order required.

Straus Family Creamery, www.strausmilk.com; organic family dairy farmers.

Toano Toy Works, www.toanotoyworks.com, Toano, VA, 877-966-3869; handcrafted, heirloom-quality wooden toys.

Tree Blocks, Tucson, AZ, 800-873-4960.

UNICEF, www.unicefusa.org, Louisiana, MO, 800-553-1200; small selection of unique play items.

USA Toy Library Association, usatla.deltacollege.org, Wilmette, IL, 847-920-9030; mesh storage bags.

Vegetarian Resource Group, www.vrg.org; wholesome baby foods from scratch.

Woodkins, www.woodkins.com; wooden play dolls of different genders and skin tones with creative clothes, accessories, and mood changes. Double Deluxe sets include Goldilocks/Red Riding Hood and Cinderella.

Other Resources from Redleaf Press

Kids Like Us: Using Persona Dolls in the Classroom
by Trisha Whitney
Kids Like Us gives teachers a tested method to introduce a new area of study, teach social or classroom skills, practice problem solving, or help children learn to empathize with others and accept differences. The author outlines five steps for using storytelling dolls to increase understanding and nurture thinking in a variety of situations.

Transition Magician: Strategies for Guiding Young Children in Early Childhood Programs
by Nola Larson, Mary Henthorne, and Barbara Plum
Offers over 200 original learning activities that will help teachers smoothly weave together everyday activities.

Transition Magician 2: More Strategies for Guiding Young Children in Early Childhood Programs
by Mary Henthorne, Nola Larson, and Ruth Chvojicek
More than 200 original learning activities, more than 50 props and games, and adaptations for toddlers and for children with special needs.

Transition Magician for Families: Helping Parents and Children with Everyday Routines
by Ruth Chvojicek, Mary Henthorne, and Nola Larson
Dozens of activity ideas for caregivers to share with families to simplify the everyday transitions outside of child care.

Infant and Toddler Experiences
by Fran Hast and Ann Hollyfield
Filled with experiences—not activities—that promote the healthiest development in infants and toddlers.

More Infant and Toddler Experiences
by Fran Hast and Ann Hollyfield
Filled with over 100 engaging new ways to fill infants' and toddlers' lives with rich experiences that reflect and celebrate each child's development.

Help Yourself! Activities to Promote Safety and Self-Esteem
by Kate Ross
Contains fun and creative ways to use the songs from the *Help Yourself!* CD as a springboard into a curriculum for promoting self-esteem and safety skills among young children.

800-423-8309
www.redleafpress.org